Cognitive Psychology
of Religion

Cognitive Psychology
of Religion

Kevin J. Eames
Covenant College

WAVELAND

PRESS, INC.

Long Grove, Illinois

For information about this book, contact:
    Waveland Press, Inc.
    4180 IL Route 83, Suite 101
    Long Grove, IL 60047-9580
    (847) 634-0081
    info@waveland.com
    www.waveland.com

This book is dedicated to our son,
Daniel Kevin Thomas Eames (2000–2013),
whose faith has become sight

Contents

    Religious Transmission
    Memorable Narratives   93
    Mental Epidemics   96
    Transmission of Counterintuitive Concepts   100
    Memes   102
    Modes of Religiosity   106
        Cognitively Optimal and Cognitively Costly
        Religious Concepts   106
        Doctrinal and Imagistic Modes of Religiosity   107
    SUMMARY 114 ⤸ NOTES 115

7   **Cognitive Aspects of Religious Rituals**   **117**
    and Experiences
    Religious Rituals: A Broad Definition   118
    Ritual and Language   121
    Ritual Form Theory   123
    Ritual Form Theory, Memory,
     and Cultural Transmission   125
    Ritual Form Theory and Modes of Religiosity   128
    SUMMARY 132 ⤸ NOTES 133

    Glossary   135
    Bibliography   145
    Index   153

Acknowledgments

What does it say about someone when they say that writing a book is a lot of fun? Perhaps that I should get out more? But it's true. I have found the time spent researching and writing this book to be a singular pleasure in my academic life. I must offer the sincerest of thanks to my colleagues at Covenant College, including Bill Davis, Jeff Hall, and Carole Yue, who encouraged me in my writing and made suggestions and corrections to a very rough and ragged manuscript. The students in my Psychology of Religion class at Covenant College also provided valuable insight, including allowing me to foist a first draft of the manuscript on them as a text. They too encouraged me by finding my text readable—high praise from undergraduate college students. Three of my undergraduate student workers, Alyssa Harmon, Megan Tures, and Sarah Woodrow, read through the final first manuscript to look for glaring errors and I am grateful to them for the time they took to do so. My wife, Lisa, and daughters, Hillary and Hannah, were patient both with the time away from them the book required, as well as the corner of the dining room table I occupied for the duration of this project. I am forever grateful for their love and support.

Theories on the Origin of Religion

QUESTIONS TO BE ADDRESSED
1. Is religion a universal human phenomenon?
2. What explains the existence of religion and the religious impulse?
3. What theories of religion involve naturalistic explanations?
4. How did anthropology initially explain the origin of religion?
5. How do contemporary evolutionary theories explain the origin of religion?
6. What theories of religion involve supernatural explanations?

Introduction: The Universality of Religion

Human beings are a religious species. Persecution, secularism, and the withering scorn of the so-called new atheism have failed to dampen the religious impulse in human beings. Not only are the world religions of Judaism, Christianity, and Islam still robust, but new religious movements continue to emerge frequently. David B. Barrett, the editor of the *World Christian Encyclopedia*, says that religion is an enormous, dynamic enterprise across the world. "It's massive, it's complex, and it's continual. We have identified nine thousand and nine hundred distinct and separate religions in the world, increasing by two or three new religions every day" (Lester, 2002). In a list entitled "A Theodiversity Sampler," Lester identifies a number of new religious movements with a significant number of members. The following are three examples from this list (Lester, 2002):

1

- *Cao Dai* is a syncretistic religion that was founded in 1926 on the principle of the common source of all religions. It has over three million members.

- The *Raelian Movement* was founded in 1973 by race car journalist Claude Vorilhon, who claimed to have had conversations with the extraterrestrials that bioengineered life on earth. The movement has around 55,000 members worldwide.

- *Umbanda* is another syncretistic religion based in Brazil with 20 million members worldwide. It combines traditional religious beliefs from Africa and South America with Catholicism and spiritualism.

Evidence from multiple disciplines suggests that religion is a human universal (Rappaport, 1999). It assumes many forms, proclaims many and conflicting beliefs, and engages in a variety of rituals. In his introduction of *The Natural History of Religion*, the Scottish philosopher David Hume allowed for the existence of an intelligent designer but noted the variety of ways in which humans have responded.

> The whole frame of nature bespeaks an intelligent author; and no rational enquirer can, after serious reflection, suspend his belief a moment with regard to the primary principles of genuine Theism and Religion. But the other question, concerning the origin of religion in human nature, is exposed to some more difficulty. The belief of invisible, intelligent power has been very generally diffused over the human race, in all places and in all ages; but it has neither perhaps been so universal as to admit of no exception, nor has it been, in any degree, uniform in the ideas, which it has suggested. (1757, p. 1)[1]

Regarding religion's pervasiveness, "anthropologists are now confident that religion is present in all human societies, even though many traditionally lack a word for religion in their own language and therefore do not separate 'religion' from other realms of culture" (Winzeler, 2012, p. 3). Anthropologists often categorize religions into four types: prehistoric religion, ancient religions, indigenous religions of small-scale societies, and world religions (Winzeler, 2012). While it would be inaccurate to see these four categories as a single linear evolutionary progression, there are common characteristics to all, including a belief in the supernatural, the sense of the sacred, and the importance of ritual as a means of embodying religious beliefs. The world religions—which include Christianity, Islam, Judaism, Buddhism, and Hinduism—are all "based in part on written texts, have lengthy known histories, and tend to be proselytizing and competitive" (Winzeler, 2012, p. 18).

How did religion(s) originate? Kunin and Miles-Watson (2006) put the responses to this question into two general categories: *transcendent* or *human*.

> One side of the dichotomy suggests that religion has its basis in a transcendent aspect of reality, however defined; the other side sug-

gests that religion arises from some aspect either of human nature or of society without reference to a transcendent source. (p. 8)

Theories in these two categories have distinct presuppositions. Theories in the transcendent category presuppose a supernatural reality often accompanied by theism, where a real God or gods are presumed to have revealed themselves to human beings. The human side assumes naturalism, where the perception of deities or the supernatural is entirely a product of human cognitive faculties. The former assumes that it is epistemologically warranted to believe in God (Plantinga, 2000), while the latter dismisses such beliefs as lacking in evidence (Dawkins, 2006). This presuppositional approach to the origin of religion is critical in understanding the direction the respective inquiries take. An approach that assumes the existence of the transcendent will not rule out supernatural explanations for phenomena; in other words, the transcendent approach does not make an *a priori* decision to exclude certain plausible explanations from all possible explanations for phenomena (Plantinga, 2007). An approach that assumes a purely naturalistic approach to the explanation of religion necessarily excludes any explanation that involves the transcendent, reducing the number of available hypotheses it will consider. Those who would adopt a naturalistic presupposition may object that transcendent explanations are not appropriate for social science inquiries and belong in a separate realm of inquiry, while others would reject the dichotomy altogether, insisting that transcendence is not a valid category for explanations of religion because it is nonexistent. Examples of origin theories based on a naturalistic presuppositions include the wish-fulfillment theories proposed by Freud and Marx (Richmond, 2010), anthropomorphism (Guthrie, 2007), or a consequence of evolution (e.g., Atran, 2002; Boyer, 2001), with more militantly Darwinian versions articulated by Dawkins (2006) and Dennett (2006).

There are also theories that begin with the presupposition of theism. Plantinga (2000) articulates a model of theism based on the theological writings of both Thomas Aquinas and John Calvin which asserts that all humans possess an innate faculty to perceive and understand God and the supernatural; this faculty is expressed by the Latin phrase *sensus divinitatis* (the sense of the divine). The Lutheran theologian Rudolf Otto asserted that religion involves a wholly other realm of experience involving the "holy" and an inexplicable encounter with the *numinous,* a unique religious experience that invokes deep emotions of awe and reverence. Expanding on Otto's ideas, the religious scholar Mircea Eliade rejected reductionist approaches to religion that sought to explain it through psychological or sociological lenses. Like Otto's idea of the holy, Eliade identified a realm of human experience involving an encounter with the sacred that offered a wholly separate dimension of reality apart from the mundane. For both Otto and Eliade, this encounter with the wholly other is not the result of false positives resulting from evolutionary adaptations, but is in fact an authentic encounter with a domain of existence that is more real and more substantive than the ordinary encounters of day-to-day existence.

◦⌇

Theories on the Origin of Religion

For the purposes of this text, we will review theories that are most relevant to understanding the cognitive science of religion. Scholarship mentioned previously (like Stewart Guthrie's anthropomorphism) will be reviewed, while the theories of Sigmund Freud and Karl Marx[2] will not.

For this first chapter, theories of the origin of religion that may be categorized as naturalistic include *intellectualism* as articulated by British anthropologists E. B. Tylor and James Frazer, *anthropomorphism* as articulated by Stewart Guthrie, and the evolutionary origins of religion as articulated by Lee Kirkpatrick, Pascal Boyer, Scot Atran, and David Sloan Wilson. Theistic approaches to the origin of religion include John Calvin's *sensus divinitatis*, Rudolph Otto's notion of the idea of the Holy, and Mircea Eliade's reality of the sacred.

◦⌇

Naturalistic Theories on the Origin of Religion

Intellectualism, Animism and Magic

Hume (1757) believed religion, specifically polytheism, originated from primitive humans' attempts to make sense out of an unpredictable and hostile world. Their ignorance of the causes of the hostile forces of nature coupled with their uncertainty about the future lead them to endow unseen powers with super-human personality, eventually conceiving of these powers in human form.

Hume's belief in the origin of religion "anticipates much of the modern intellectualist position" (Guthrie, 2007, p. 42), most notably voiced by Edward Burnett Tylor and James Frazer, early proponents of an anthropological explanation for religion.

Boyer (2001) notes that the central assumption of intellectualism assumes that "if a phenomenon is common to human experience and people do not have the conceptual means to understand it, then they will try and find some speculative explanation" (p. 15). Both Tylor and Frazer found evidence in the origin of religion in the mistaken attributions made by primitive humans who were trying to make sense of their worlds.

E. B. Tylor and Animism

E. B. Tylor was one of the first modern anthropologists to suggest that religion emerged out of a human tendency to attribute spiritual essence to both animate and inanimate things. Though Tylor was considered an anthropologist, he did most of his work in the privacy of his study, as opposed to the field work done by anthropologists who followed. He wrote a seminal two-volume classic that addressed religion and culture. In the second volume of *Primitive Culture* (1871), Tylor offered a straightforward definition of religion which served as a basis for elaboration among those who followed him: religion involves the belief in Spiritual Beings. According to Tylor, the one common attribute characterized by all religions is "the belief in spirits who think, act, and feel like human persons" (Pals, 2006, p. 26). This belief in spiritual beings is embedded in a doctrine Tylor labels as *animism,* which Stark (2007) describes as "the belief that literally everything is inhabited by a spirit, not only animate things, but inanimate things as well" (p. 27). Since animism characterizes the beliefs of primitive culture, Tylor (1871) believed that "animism characterizes tribes very low in the scale of humanity" (p. 426) and that these early primitive beliefs were sufficient to form the roots of more sophisticated religions, "for where the root is, the branches will generally be produced" (p. 426).

In applying animism to primitive religions, Tylor contradicts the notion that native practitioners are practicing idol worship in the reverence of certain sacred objects: "They do not worship sticks and stones; they adore the anima within, the spirit which . . . gives the wood of the stick or substance of the stone its life and power" (Pals, 2006, pp. 27–28). For Tylor, animism consists of two parts: (1) the belief that individuals possess a soul which continues after death, and (2) the existence of spirits "upward to the rank of powerful deities" (Tylor, 1871, p. 426). The belief in powerful deities also suggests the superintendence of these deities over mortal beings both in this life and the next, and that these deities respond with either pleasure or displeasure to the behaviors of humans and therefore provoke acts of reverence and atonement for perceived wrongs committed. Moreover, Tylor goes on to divide these spirits into two categories: "spirits occupied in affecting for good and ill the life of Man, and spirits especially concerned in carrying on the operations of Nature" (1871, p. 185).

As an intellectual product of the 19th century, Tylor was likely influenced by Hegel's *Phenomenology of Geist* (1806), which, among other things, saw the process of cultural maturation as a progression "from animism to polytheism to a monotheism of wrath to a monotheism of love" (Davis, 2014). Inasmuch as Hegel's work emphasized the logic of development as informing all things, it follows that a culture can be evaluated on the basis of its religion to determine its maturity. Since this view was pervasive throughout Europe in the 19th century, Tylor and others saw themselves as the possessors of a mature, enlightened culture that had the responsibility to "parent" more primitive cultures through colonialism, which was favored as a means of civilizing them.

Corresponding with Hegel's notion of an internal logic of develop- ment underlying biological reality, Darwin's theory of evolution also debuted into the intellectual zeitgeist of the 19th century, which others quickly sought to apply to other aspects of the human experience, includ- ing culture and religion (Kunin & Miles-Watson, 2006). As such, Tylor believed that, like other aspects of human culture, animism grew and developed as it spread among practitioners through a kind of intellectual evolution. Deities specifically associated with individual entities like a specific tree soon developed into the deity of all trees, implying that the deity was not constrained to that particular location but able to travel (Pals, 2006). As beliefs about animism became more sophisticated, com- plex hierarchies of deities developed, ultimately culminating in the one supreme deity characteristic of Judaism, Christianity, and Islam (Pals, 2006). As complex and sophisticated as the theologies of the world reli- gions became, Tylor believed "that animism at bottom is a grand mis- take" (Pals, 2006, p. 30) that nonetheless spawned the growth and development of religions both tribal and worldwide. In light of these speculations, Tylor believed theologians must acknowledge that the doc- trines to which they adhere are in fact not original to their particular faith, but are rooted in a common animism that has branched into each particular religion.

Tylor is among those anthropologists who practice an *intellectualist* approach to the study of religion (Pals, 2006). By "intellectualist," Pals means that Tylor believed religion resulted from beliefs that individuals derived from trying to make sense of the world. Religion "is thought to originate in the mind of the individual 'savage philosopher,' as Tylor calls him, the lone prehistoric thinker who tries to solve the riddles of life and then passes on his interests and ideas to others" (Pals, 2006, p. 46).

James Frazer and Magic

Like Tylor, James Frazer conducted his anthropological exploration of religion in his study. In Frazer's seminal work, *The Golden Bough: A Study in Magic and Religion* (1890), he asserts that religion originates from a primitive conceptualization of *magic*. Magic is based on a flawed interpre- tation of certain principles of association in the natural world; that is, "when two things can in some way be mentally associated—when in the mind they appear 'sympathetic'—they must also be physically associated in the outside world" (Pals, 2006, p. 36).

These *laws of association* to which Frazer refers are rooted in British empiricism and Locke's "association of ideas" articulated in his *Essay Concerning Human Understanding* (1690). The American psychologist How- ard C. Warren defines the two laws of association as follows:

> The Law of Contiguity is generally stated in substantially the follow- ing terms: "A sensation or idea tends to recall other experiences

which formerly occurred in close proximity to it." The Law of Similarity is generally formulated as follows: "An experience tends to
recall experiences which resemble it." (1921, p. 283)

It is these laws which Frazer believed to be "excellent in themselves and
indeed absolutely essential to the working of the human mind." (Frazer,
1890).

Frazer uses the more refined term *sympathetic magic* to describe the
associations that primitive people made about their environment. Frazer
further refines sympathetic magic into two categories that correspond with
the laws of association described above. Frazer describes them this way:

First, like produces like, or that an effect resembles its cause; and second, that things which have once been in contact with each other
continue to act on each other at a distance after the physical contact
has been severed. (1890)

Those who understood these principles at the *folk psychology* (or naïve)
level became magicians. The magician believed that he could "produce any
effect he desire[d] merely by imitating it," (Frazer, 1890) thus employing
the law of similarity. The magician could also infer from the law of conti-
guity "that whatever he does to a material object will affect equally the
person with whom the object was once in contact" (Frazer, 1890).

Frazer believes that the emergence of religion served as a kind of
bridge between magic and science. Magic was fatally flawed by its misapplication of the principles of association. Of these laws of association,
Frazer writes that "legitimately applied they yield science; illegitimately
applied they yield magic, the bastard sister of science. . . . All magic is
necessarily false and barren; for were it ever to become true and fruitful,
it would no longer be magic but science" (Frazer, 1890). Since magic had
shown itself to be bankrupt and powerless, Frazer believes "mankind
cast about for a truer theory of nature and a more fruitful method of tun-
ing her resources to account" (Frazer, 1890).

Inasmuch as magic was an attempt by humans to exercise control
over their environment by misapplying the laws of association, religion
emerges out of magic as an attempt to exercise control over the deities
who themselves control nature and the lives of humans. For Frazer, the
exercise of religion involves winning the favor of those deities; in the earlier history of religion, the role of the priest and magician overlapped.
Religious exercises like prayer and sacrifice were practiced to appease
angry deities, while incantations were recited with the hope of manipulating natural forces.

Like Tylor, Frazer's approach to religion is dependent on a theory of
intellectual evolution, which assumes that religious beliefs evolve from
local, tribal deities with limited power to more sophisticated pantheons
to monotheism. These evolutionary presuppositions became problematic
when contemporary critics of Frazer and Tylor noted that monotheism,

hypothetically an advanced form of religion, was more common among the primitive hunter-gatherer cultures than among agricultural cultures, which were considered more advanced (Pals, 2006).

A final criticism involves the anthropological method both Tylor and Frazer used to forge their theories. The early 20th century perspective was largely ethnocentric, assuming the superiority of the West's perspective on science and religion and failing to take into account how the indigenous peoples themselves viewed their religious beliefs. Kunin and Miles-Watson critiqued *The Golden Bough* for bringing "together wide ranges of unrelated data, which often arise from unreliable or problematic sources" (2006, p. 44). As objective as Frazer might have tried to be, his deductive approach resulted in a confirmation bias that sought out otherwise disparate data that supported his hypotheses.

The value of the intellectualist approach taken by Tylor and Frazer is in its suggestion that human beings apply their cognitive faculties to make sense of and explain their world. Though Tylor and Frazer assert that these cognitive faculties led primitive people into erroneous assumptions about their world, it does not necessarily follow that all assumptions derived from human cognitive faculties about the supernatural world are faulty. Moreover, the universality of the human desire to find overarching explanations for phenomena could be evidence that human beings are innately motivated to explore the big picture of meaning and purpose. If this is true, then science and religion spring from the same basic human motivation (Davis, 2014).

Anthropomorphism and Interpretive Mistakes

Stewart Guthrie extends the work of Tylor by asserting that religion originates from the human tendency to mistakenly attribute *agency* to natural phenomena, where agency is defined as that which permits an entity to act by their own volition and not mechanically in response to some external stimulus, like a billiard ball struck by the cue ball (Barrett, 2004). The false attribution of agency amounts to *anthropomorphism*, which Guthrie defines as "the attribution of human features to nonhuman things and events" (1996, p. 416). Guthrie goes on to assert that:

> religion, like secular thought and action, anthropomorphize the world of phenomena. That is, we invoke its humanlike beings—its gods—not in a vacuum, but to account for particular things and events . . . we hear noises in the wind as voices, see shadows as lurking figures, and see patterns in nature as design. (1996, p. 416)

The tendency to anthropomorphize is not restricted to religious contexts. Once the voices have been determined to be noises or the lurking figures determined to be shadows, we realize our mistake. "When we think plagues and earthquakes are the action of gods—we make the same mistake" (Guthrie, 1996, p. 416).

These mistakes, or false positives, are perceptual and conceptual mistakes that arise from "our scanning an uncertain world for what matters most" (Guthrie, 2007, p. 37). Guthrie believes the ease with which we can attribute agency to ambiguous phenomena has to do with survival: "when we are right in those interpretations, we gain important information, and when we are wrong we lose relatively little" (2007, p. 37).

According to Guthrie, attribution of agency occurs when we perceive an entity as having the "capacity for intention, goal-directedness, and corresponding action" (2007, p. 46). These characteristics are not directly observable but must be imputed to the entity to which agency is attributed. The ability to make such imputations forms our folk psychology, otherwise known as *theory of mind* (Barrett, 2011). Theory of mind (ToM) is an innate, unconsciously employed cognitive device humans use to interpret the thoughts, intentions, and actions of others in terms of their unobservable minds, which are in turn considered separately from the bodies they inhabit (Guthrie, 2007). This intuitive dualism (that appears to be innate) suggests that "minds are separable from bodies, and the category of agent is large and open-ended, extending even to biologically inanimate objects" (Guthrie, 2007, p. 49). As such, humans are likely to attribute motives, desires, and intentions to objects or entities in their environment that are likely candidates to have minds. When a tree with branches waving vigorously in the wind seems "angry," that attribution requires an assumption of emotion (anger) and intention (clouting someone), and the vigorous waving is designed to induce the appropriate response—either appeasement or being left alone. Moreover, such an attribution also allows for the presence of some spiritual essence in the tree, similar to human minds, given the human tendency to attribute agency to minds that exist apart from the bodies (or trees) they inhabit.

For Guthrie, the human tendency to hear voices in the wind as traces of invisible agents are inevitable consequences of how we process environmental information. While Guthrie allows that other categories of theories allow for the benefits of religion, including the emotional comfort derived from wish-fulfillment or the benefits of social solidarity religion offers, religion is ultimately the result of mistaken attributions of agency derived from the intuitive use of theory of mind. Because this innate tendency is an adaptive mechanism protecting us against predators and promoting survival, it is a mistake Guthrie believes will "inevitably arise again and again" (2007, p. 56).

∽

Evolutionary Approaches to Religion

Most of the approaches to explain the origin of religion begin with naturalistic assumptions, meaning appeals to anything extra-natural—as with alchemy, witchcraft and elements of many major religions, or supernatural revelation—are excluded. Some theories explicitly use evolution as an explanatory framework, though this has been a relatively recent development. Wilson and Green (2007) note that, while Darwin was interested in applying evolutionary theory to all aspects of human life, including religion, the theory proper remained confined to the biological sciences. This was because attempts to appropriate Darwin's theory to explain the evolution of culture in linear, upward progression (as Tylor and Frazer attempted to do) were ultimately unsuccessful as field research in anthropology failed to support it. Wilson and Green (2007) identify the publication of E. O. Wilson's book *Sociobiology* in 1975 as a significant step toward a valid explanation of the social aspects of human evolution. They write that, apart from the social Darwinism of the early 20th century, a more sophisticated approach to human evolution is a recent phenomenon: "to give an idea of its recency, terms such as 'evolutionary psychology' and 'evolutionary anthropology' were not even coined until the 1980s and 90s" (p. 2). Extending these integrative approaches to the study of religion, Wilson and Green are among several scholars who constitute a school of thought called *evolutionary religious studies.*

Evolutionary approaches to the origins of religion typically view religion as an evolutionary by-product of brain functions that are more appropriate for nonreligious contexts (Wilson & Green, 2007). Some contend that religion is a *spandrel*, a notion first suggested by evolutionary biologist Stephen J. Gould (Gould & Lewontin, 1979). A spandrel is an architectural term describing outcomes that weren't intended but were by-products of necessary architectural structures. "For example, supporting a dome with four arches necessarily creates triangular spaces ('spandrels') in the corners, where two arches meet at right angles" (Grantham, 2004, p. 39).

The arrow indicates an example of a spandrel.

Although the paper itself has been criticized (e.g., Fox, 2011), the concept of spandrels has come to serve as a cogent illustration of the hypothesis that humans are not innately religious, but that religion is a derivative of some other cognitive process.

Attachment and the Evolution of Religion

Lee Kirkpatrick proposes that John Bowlby's attachment theory explains religion "as a collection of by-products of numerous specialized psychological systems that evolved over the course of human history for other (i.e., nonreligious) functions" (2005, p. viii). According to Kirkpatrick, Bowlby's (1980) attachment theory is an adaptive mechanism "for the purpose of maintaining proximity between helpless infants and their primary caregivers . . . for protection against predators and other environmental dangers" (Kirkpatrick, 2005, p. 336). The attachment process produces affectional bonds between infant and caregiver which later affects the development of romantic pair-bonding (Kirkpatrick & Shaver, 1990). Forming affectional bonds is one of many social-cognitive processes designed to promote survival for both individuals and groups. Other such processes include recognition of kin and participation in ingroups, formation of coalitions, mutually beneficial altruism, and rules for social reciprocity (Kirkpatrick, 2005). These, Kirkpatrick contends, provide the psychological foundation for forming attachments with supernatural agents.

> The operation of each of these social-cognitive systems, along with the attachment system, is evident in diverse ways across religions. Gods and other supernatural beings might be treated psychologically as attachment figures, but also . . . as kin (e.g., ancestors or Father), coalitional partners ("God is on our side"), social-exchange partners (who offer particular provisions in exchange for proper behavior, sacrifices, etc.), or high-status "leaders" (God as "king"). (Kirkpatrick, 2005, pp. 339–340)

The Cognitive Science of Religion

The cognitive science of religion is a multidisciplinary field of scholarship that draws from cognitive psychology, anthropology, sociology, and linguistics to offer naturalistic explanations for the origin of religion. The predominant view of the cognitive science of religion is that religion is an unintended by-product that has evolved as a result of human cognitive architecture. This view is called the *standard model* (Jensen, 2009). Prominent scholars in this area include Scott Atran, Pascal Boyer, and Ilkka Pyysiäinen, among others. Alternatives to the standard model include *selectionist models* that accept that "various aspects of religion originated as by-products of evolved cognitive structures but were subsequently co-opted for adaptive purposes" (Powell & Clarke, 2012, p. 457).

Boyer's (2001) cognitive science of religion involves "a number of cognitive systems working in concert [to] produce a general natural *disposition* for humans to embrace belief in gods of one sort or another" (Clark & Barrett, 2010, p. 179). Boyer believes religion originates from the way the human brain makes inferences about phenomena that involve supernatural explanations. Successful religious ideas are transmitted through cultural *memes*, a concept Richard Dawkins likens to genes at the cultural level. "Memes are units of culture: notions, values, stories, etc. that get people to speak or act in certain ways that make other people store a replicated version of these mental units" (Boyer, 2001, p. 35). Using an epidemiological model of cultural transmission from Sperber (1996), Boyer contends that the most successful memes spread like contagion causing cultural epidemics. "To explain religion is to explain a particular kind of mental epidemic whereby people develop (on the basis of variable information) rather similar forms of religious concepts and norms" (Boyer, 2001, p. 47). Which religious ideas are most likely to be successful and spread? Those "that (1) are easily and readily represented by human cognitive equipment, (2) are attention-demanding regardless of cultural conditions, (3) have rich 'inferential potential' such that they readily generate inferences, explanations, and predictions relevant to many domains of human concern, and (4) motivate actions that reinforce belief, i.e., they matter" (Clark & Barrett, 2010, p. 180).

Like Boyer, Scott Atran also approaches the origin of religion as an evolutionary by-product. However, "because there is no such entity as 'religion,' it makes no sense to ask how 'it' evolved" (Atran, 2002, p. 15). Instead, religious belief and practice emerge out of specific body and brain systems that are designed to detect agents like predators or prey. The supernatural agents that typically populate religions emerge from a cognitive mechanism that is "trip-wired to attribute agency to virtually any action that mimics the stimulus conditions of natural agents" (Atran, 2002, p. 35).

While the previously mentioned theories would see religion "as a by-product (or "spandrel") of genetic or cultural evolution," David Sloan Wilson views religion "as group-level adaptation" (Wilson, 2002, p. 43). In his book *Darwin's Cathedral* (2002), Wilson contends that religion is the consequence of an adaptive evolutionary process at the group level (versus the individual level) designed to promote ingroup cooperation. His hypothesis treats religions as organisms and therefore products of natural selection. "Through countless generations of variation and selection, they acquire properties that enable them to survive and reproduce in their environments" (Wilson, 2002, p. 1). For Wilson, cultural transmission "enables the evolution of effective groups without requiring that genetic adaptations do all the work" (Bulbulia & Frean, 2009, p. 177). What makes Wilson's view of the evolutionary origins of religion different from the theories of Kirkpatrick, Boyer, and Atran is that Wilson believes *religion itself is adaptive* and not an adaptive by-product of some other nonreligious function. Wilson offers several historic examples of the secular utility of religion. One such example involves the worship of Dewi Danu, goddess of the waters of the island of Bali. Worship is centered in a colossal temple that stands on the summit of a volcano. As rainwater cascades down the mountain, a series of smaller temples, dedicated to other deities, direct the water into aqueducts that irrigate the rice fields. The hierarchical structure of the priests selected to serve the goddess in her temple coupled with the complex irrigation system that requires cooperation and oversight for those it serves demonstrates "that the water temple system functions adaptively to coordinate the activities of thousands of farmers over an area of hundreds of square kilometers" (Wilson, 2002, p. 129). Judaism is a second example Wilson provides in demonstrating the secular utility of religion. Of the Ten Commandments, Wilson says, "it is almost embarrassingly obvious that groups who obey these rules will function well as adaptive units, compared to groups that do not" (Wilson, 2002, p. 133). Wilson argues that two aspects of Judaism as articulated in the Old Testament were notably adaptive for the survival of the religion: first, biological success is commanded in the instruction to be fruitful and multiply; second, the Old Testament provided two sets of laws, one for how they would treat one another, and the other for how they would treat members of other groups, with the ingroup laws designed to promote charity and harmony and the outgroup laws varied according to the context. In some cases the alien was treated with charity while in others they were destroyed (Wilson, 2002).

Theistic Approaches to the Origin of Religion

Theistic approaches to theories of the origin of religion begin with two presuppositions. The first is recognition of an innate *faculty* that allows humans to perceive and comprehend, on some level, the supernatural, specifically God and the sacred. Following this, it is therefore warranted to expand the evidence base beyond the constraints provided by naturalism (Plantinga, 2011). The argument for a theistic approach is best articulated by the contemporary philosopher Alvin Plantinga (2007):

> In investigating a given subject or topic, one should use all that one knows. My neighbor's lawn is full of dandelions; I want to learn why. There are many avenues of investigation: I can take soil analyses, try to find out how many dandelions there were last year, look to see if there are large numbers of dandelions in the yards on either side—and the like; and of course all of this is relevant. But suppose my neighbor has also told me that he purposely planted them (he really likes the color yellow); it would be folly for me to refuse to consider that bit of what I know in my investigation. In conducting any inquiry or investigation, obviously, I should employ everything I know, all the relevant information I have. For if I employ only part of what I know, omitting something relevant, I may very well come out with an inadequate or even wholly mistaken answer. The principle involved here is simple, and, I should have thought, uncontroversial: one should use all one's (relevant) evidence in any investigation. (p. 32)

Aquinas, Calvin, and *Sensus Divinitatis*

Plantinga (2000) articulates a model of theism he terms the *Aquinas/Calvin model* of theistic belief. This model is so titled because both the

Roman Catholic theologian Thomas Aquinas (1225–1274) and the Protestant reformer John Calvin (1509–1564) believed that all humans possess an innate knowledge and awareness of God. It is noteworthy that
these eminent theologians from very different and often opposing traditions would agree on such a foundational belief, and, as Plantinga notes,
"anything on which Calvin and Aquinas are in accord is something to
which we had better pay careful attention" (Plantinga, 2000, p. 170). In
his *Summa Theologica*, Aquinas writes, "There is a certain general and con-
fused knowledge of God, which is in almost all men." Calvin elaborates
on this in the *Institutes of the Christian Religion*, where he argued that
"there is within the human mind, and indeed by natural instinct, an
awareness of divinity" (1960, p. 43), which God himself implanted in all
human beings. This awareness of divinity is typically referred to by the
Latin phrase *sensus divinitatis*. This *sensus divinitatis* provides the foundation for all religions. In response to the objection that religion is a human
device invented by some to exercise power through fear over other, more
gullible people, Calvin argues that while:

> clever men have devised very many things in religion by which to
> inspire the common folk with reverence and to strike them with ter-
> ror . . . they would never have achieved this if men's minds had not
> already been imbued with a firm conviction about God, from which
> the inclination toward religion springs as from a seed. (1960, p. 45)

Plantinga (2000) interprets the Aquinas/Calvin model as identifying
a kind of "faculty or cognitive mechanism, what Calvin calls a *sensus divinitatis* or sense of divinity, which in a wide variety of circumstances produces in us beliefs about God" (p. 172). These beliefs occur intuitively,
similarly to the beliefs we hold in what we perceive and what we remember. A person seeing a red flower doesn't infer that belief, it occurs intuitively and innately as a consequence of the faculty for sight. Plantinga
(2000) further defines this *sensus divinitatis* as "a disposition or set of dis-
positions to form theistic beliefs in various circumstances, in response to
the sorts of conditions or stimuli that trigger the working of this sense of
divinity" (p. 173).

Central to understanding Calvin's notion of *sensus divinitatis* is the
tendency for humans to suppress, distort, or deny it. Drawing from
Augustine of Hippo's notion of original sin, Calvin believed this knowledge of God is suppressed or corrupted by superstition, pride, and hypoc-
risy. In the strong language typical of Calvin in the *Institutes*, he wrote:

> For the blindness under which they labor is almost always mixed
> with proud vanity and obstinacy. Indeed, vanity joined with pride
> can be detected from the fact that, in seeking God, miserable men do
> not rise about themselves as they should, but measure him by the
> yardstick of their own carnal stupidity, and neglect sound investiga-
> tion; thus out of curiosity they fly off into empty speculation. They do

not therefore apprehend God as he offers himself, but imagine him as they have fashioned him in their own presumption. (1960, p. 47)

Clark and Barrett (2010) note that, while Plantinga's view of the *sensus divinitatis* is derived from Calvin's, it also differs from Calvin's. Calvin's *sensus divinitatis* is an innate faculty existent from birth that equips us to simply and easily believe in a Creator endowed with omniscience, omnipotence, and omnipresence; such beliefs were not dependent on experience. Moreover, Calvin believed that the *sensus divinitatis* allowed us to perceive God in His creation. "One, whether peasant or physiologist or physicist, can quite simply see the order and symmetry of the cosmos and human person and so become aware of the being on whom that order and symmetry depend" (Clark & Barrett, 2010, p. 175). Plantinga differs from Calvin in that Plantinga's *sensus divinitatis* involves experience. He "argues that belief in God is produced in response to a variety of widely realized circumstances such as moments of guilt, gratitude, or a sense of God's handiwork in nature" (Clark & Barrett, 2010, p. 175).

Clark and Barrett (2011) themselves juxtapose the arguments from the cognitive science of religion with philosophical arguments of Thomas Reid, whose Scottish common sense approach calls for trust in the immediate, intuitive data perceived through normal cognitive faculties. They argue that empirical research in the cognitive science of religion suggests that a *sensus divinitatis* is an emergent faculty, a naturally occurring "god-faculty" that is as trustworthy as other naturally occurring faculties. They describe the god-faculty as "the ordinary arrangement and function of cognitive architecture in human minds [that] often produces nonreflective, unreasoned belief in gods" where "gods" are "any supernatural intentional agents whose existence would impinge upon human activity" (p. 14). Clark and Barrett (2011) rely on empirical evidence to support the suggestion of the god-faculty, drawing on much of the empirical research supporting the theories cited previously (e.g., Guthrie, Boyer, Atran). Examples include empirical support for the tendency toward intuitive belief in dualism (e.g., mind and body separation) suggested by Bering (2002) and Bloom (2004) and children's tendency to attribute purpose and intent to natural phenomenon, like believing rocks are pointy so animals won't sit on them (Kelemen, 2004). Nonetheless, the empirical support for the god-faculty fundamentally differs from the *sensus divinitatis* of Calvin, Reid, and Plantinga. The naturalistic approaches assume the god-faculty results from evolutionary adaptations that inadvertently produced the spandrel of agency detection and belief in the supernatural. "Neither Calvin nor Plantinga treat belief in God as an evolutionary spandrel as suggested by those who offer evolutionary accounts. . . . Belief in God is the direct and intended product of the god-faculty, not an epiphenomenal by-product of an agency detecting device" (Clark & Barrett, 2010, p. 185).

The Holy and the Sacred

The theologian Rudolph Otto (1869–1937) articulated a similar notion of the *sensus divinitatis* in his understanding of the "Holy." Otto would not agree that such a faculty is an evolutionary by-product, but an authentic capacity for perception of the holy. In his book *The Idea of the Holy* (1958), Otto describes the human faculty for perceiving and experiencing the Holy, or what he termed the *numinous*. "It is this faculty in relation with the transcendent that forms the basis of religion" (Kunin & Miles-Watson, 2006, p. 78). What distinguishes Otto's idea is its recognition that a reliance on rational explanations of God are incomplete, lacking in a wholly separate category that involves the *ineffable*, or that which is profound, overwhelming, and inexpressible. Otto coined the term *numinous* to describe this ineffable state of mind that is "perfectly *sui generis* and irreudiclbe to any other; and therefore, like very absolutely primary and elementary datum, while it admits of being discussed, it cannot be strictly defined" (p. 7). Moreover, this state of mind cannot be taught to others, "it can only be evoked, awakened in the mind, as everything that comes 'of the spirit' must be awakened" (Otto, 2006, p. 82).

This encounter with the numinous is winsomely illustrated in the children's book *The Wind in the Willows* by Kenneth Grahame (1908). While searching for a missing otter pup, Mole, one of the book's main characters, finds him curled up asleep at the feet of Pan. Grahame describes how Mole felt in the presence of this woodland-creature deity:

> Then suddenly the Mole felt a great Awe fall upon him, an awe that turned his muscles to water, bowed his head, and rooted his feet to the ground. It was no panic terror—indeed he felt wonderfully at peace and happy—but it was an awe that smote and held him and, without seeing, he knew it could only mean that some august Presence was very, very near. (p. 154)

Otto's reliance on the ineffability of the numinous experience does run counter to both the theistic and atheistic cognitive science of religion approaches, which contend that the god-faculty is an ordinary part of human cognitive architecture that makes belief in and experience with God possible and accessible.

Like Otto, Mircea Eliade believed there was something unique and separate about the religious domain. From tribal religions to the great world religions, there is a separation between the sacred and the profane. The profane involves the common, everyday experiences of life; it is transient, fragile, and chaotic (Pals, 2006). Conversely, the sacred is a transcendent domain of experience that is wholly unlike the profane; it is eternal, powerful, and monumental—a place populated with heroes, spirits, and gods (Pals, 2006).

> In an encounter with the sacred . . . people feel in touch with something otherworldly in character; they feel they have brushed against a

reality unlike all others they know, a dimension of existence that is alarmingly powerful, strangely different, surpassingly real and enduring. (Pals, 2006, p. 200)

For Eliade, the sacred was not the product of a flawed interpretation of associated events attributed to magic, as James Frazer (1890) might suggest, but a genuine domain of human existence accessible to all. The role of religion, regardless of creed, is to promote encounters with the sacred (Pals, 2006).

SUMMARY

- Religion in its many forms appears to be a human universal (e.g., Rappaport, 1999).
- Explanations for the origin of religion may be grouped into two major categories: transcendent and human (Kunin & Miles-Watson, 2006). Transcendent subsumes theistic explanations of the origin of religion, while naturalism may be used as a synonym for human explanations.
- A common theme among naturalistic explanations for religion is, as David Hume (1757) noted, an attempt to make sense out of an unpredictable and dangerous world.
- E. B. Tylor (1871) was an early proponent of a naturalistic approach to religion, believing that religion emerged from primitive humans' mistaken attribution of *animism*, the belief that all things animate and inanimate are indwelt by spirits.
- James Frazer (Frazer, 1890) was also an early proponent of a naturalistic approach to religion, believing that religion emerged from primitive humans' application of magic. Magic resulted from a naïve application of the laws of association, resulting in religion. This application was flawed because it yielded belief in the supernatural. Appropriately applied, the laws of association would yield science.
- Tylor and Frazer are considered proponents of the intellectualist approach to the origin of religion.
- Stewart Guthrie (1996) attributes mistakes in interpreting natural phenomena as supernatural and anthropomorphizing them into deities.
- Lee Kirkpatrick (2005) attributes religion to the combination effects of attachment and the social-cognitive mechanisms designed to promote group survival.
- Pascal Boyer (2001) and Scott Atran (2002) see religion as a vestigial by-product of other cognitive mechanisms needed for adapting to a hostile environment. This is typically called the standard model of the cognitive science of religion.

- David Sloan Wilson (2002) believes religion is an evolutionary adaptation that allows for survival and cooperation at the group level.
- Guthrie, Kirkpatrick, Boyer, Atran, and Wilson provide naturalistic explanations for religion.
- Alvin Plantinga (2000) believes the explanation for religion is best explained by the Aquinas/Calvin model, which depends on the *sensus divinitatis*, or awareness of divinity. It is this awareness of divinity that promotes the belief in and practice of religion.
- Rudolph Otto (1958) believes humans have a faculty for sensing and experiencing the numinous, which permits us to experience a reality that is profound, overwhelming, and inexpressible. These experiences provide the foundation for religion.
- Mircea Eliade differentiated between the sacred and the profane, acknowledging the latter to be transient and fragile while the former is eternal, powerful, and monumental (Pals, 2006). Like Otto, Eliade believed the sacred existed as an experiential category wholly apart from the natural, day-to-day experiences of living.

NOTES

[1] Accessed from http://oll.libertyfund.org/titles/340

[2] Daniel L. Pals in *Eight Theories of Religion, 2nd Edition* (2006) explores theories of religion held by Freud, Durkheim, Marx, and Weber, among others.

2

Neuroscience and Religious Belief

QUESTIONS TO BE ADDRESSED

1. Which areas of the brain become active when individuals have a religious experience or engage in religious activities?
2. Does current brain imaging technology provide an adequate basis for determining a causal relationship between brain activity and religious activity?
3. To what extent is activity in the temporal lobe associated with epilepsy relate to religious/mystical experiences?
4. Can a mystical experience, specifically a sensed presence, be induced externally through transcranial magnetic stimulation designed to approximate temporal lobe activity?
5. What is neurotheology and on what empirical foundations is this field of scholarship based?
6. What distinct cognitive neural network patterns have been experimentally associated with religious experiences?
7. How does the brain respond at the neural level to different forms of prayer?
8. What are some of the limitations of using brain imaging technology to correlate brain activity and religiosity?

Introduction

It should come as no surprise to us that when we engage in activities or have experiences, our brain is active. Whether it is watching a tennis match, performing a routine mathematical calculation, driving to a familiar place, or praying, there is a correlating amount of cerebral blood flow providing the energy to the parts of the brain most involved with the activity or experience. Similarly, when we are running to catch a bus, blood flows to the large muscles in our legs to provide the energy they need to run.

Advances in imaging technology have provided opportunities to observe the brain in action. PET (positron emission tomography) and SPECT (single-photon emission computed tomography) scans use radioactive isotopes to detect blood flow in specific areas of the brain, while fMRI (functional magnetic resonance imaging) takes advantage of the blood's magnetic properties, showing active parts of the brain that contain higher concentrations of oxygenated blood (Galotti, 2013). These techniques show what parts of the brain "light up" when they are active. But what do those parts that light up tell us about what is actually happening in the person's mind? Technologies like fMRI do not reveal specific thoughts or feelings; "they can only tell that brain regions already known to be associated with certain thoughts or feelings have demonstrated an increase in activity—hence the proper term 'neural correlates' for the colorful dabs on brain scans" (Satel & Lilienfeld, 2013, p. 3).

Satel and Lilienfeld's use of the term *neural correlates* is significant for two reasons. First, certain neural activity corresponds with certain mental or physical activity. For example, fMRI scans showed that different parts of the brain were active depending on the type of prayer in which participants were praying (Schjoedt, 2009). Informal, conversational prayer activated different regions of the brain than formal, ritualized prayer. Second, these phenomena are correlates, meaning the mental or physical activity occurs together with the neural activity, but the former doesn't necessarily cause the latter; the scientific evidence does not demonstrate causation. Mascelko (2013) notes that "from a scientific perspective, we do not know whether any observed neural activity during a religious experience is the actual cause of the experience, a marker of it, or a consequence" (p. 205).

What then is the relationship between neuroscience and religion? Those who study the relationship are interested in "what happens in the brain when someone engages in an activity or has an experience that is labeled religious or spiritual" (Mascelko, 2013, p. 205). This line of inquiry seeks to match the particular religious experience with specific lobes and/or areas in the brain. Before examining the specific research, it would be helpful to briefly review key components of the brain.

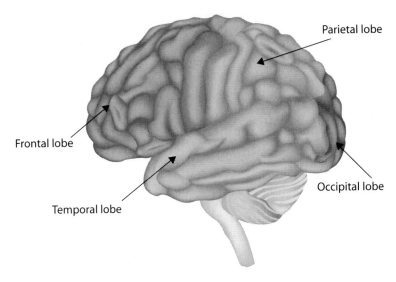

Cerebral cortex

The cerebral cortex, the top layer of the brain, is divided into four lobes: the frontal lobe, which contains the prefrontal cortex, an area involved in executive function, decision-making, and planning; the parietal lobe, which processes sensory information, including a person's sense of self; the temporal lobes, which process auditory information and facial recognition; and the occipital lobe, which processes visual information (Galotti, 2013). Another important brain structure is the limbic system, which contains areas involved with short-term memory (the hippocampus), strong emotion and the fight-flight response (the amygdala), and regulation of basic bodily needs like hunger and thirst (the hypothalamus) (Galotti, 2013). Neuroscientists interested in how religion affects these areas will observe them using one or more of the scanning technologies described above. Colored areas indicate an increase in blood flow, indicating the need for oxygen and glucose to sustain the energy required for those areas of the brain to function. When the prefrontal cortex is active, for example, an fMRI scan shows that area to be infused with red; when the prefrontal cortex is inactive, the fMRI scan shows that area to be dark.

Temporal Lobe Epilepsy: The Sacred Disease?

Research on the neural correlates of religious experiences can be grouped into two categories: (1) extraordinary or mystical experiences, like visions or states of ecstasy and (2) ordinary, routine experiences like conversational prayer or hymn-singing (Mascelko, 2013). Among religious experiences that are exotic or mystical, those associated with temporal lobe epilepsy (TLE) have received considerable attention from researchers interested in neural correlates of religion. Epilepsy, a disease characterized by uncontrollable seizures resulting from dysregulation of electrical activity in the brain, was considered by the ancient Greeks to be "the sacred disease" (Hood, Hill, & Spilka, 2009) because the episodes can be accompanied by changes in perception, hallucinations, and heightened religiosity. While the association with religiosity and epilepsy is acknowledged, Hood et al. note that such an association is "complex, unclear, and generally weak" (p. 62).

TLE continues to be the subject of inquiry regarding its relationship with religion. Dewhurst and Beard (1970) reported on six patients with TLE who experienced sudden religious conversion. In a study of Japanese TLE patients, Ogata and Miyakawa (1998) reported on three cases of post-seizure psychosis accompanied by transcendent religious experiences, all involving visual or auditory hallucinations and altered states of consciousness. All three of the patients had previously been involved in various forms of religiosity like Buddhism, Christianity, or various folk religions indigenous to Japan, and had had religious experiences prior to the onset of the episode under study. The seizures and psychotic episodes that followed appeared to amplify existing religiosity, augmenting it with religious hallucinations.

∽

Michael Persinger's God Helmet

Consistent with the TLE theory of religiosity, psychologist Michael Persinger contends that religious experiences may be attributed to transient, epileptic-like electrical activity in the temporal lobe, though such experiences occur without the convulsions associated with epilepsy. Persinger (1984) identified epileptic-like electrical activity in the temporal lobes of a single practitioner of transcendental meditation during a meditation episode and a single member of a Pentecostal Christian church during prolonged period of intermittent episodes of speaking in tongues (*glossolalia*). The association between religious activity and electrical activity in the temporal lobe approximating epilepsy is, according to Persinger, evidence of the origins of religiosity in humans. In addition to the association between temporal lobe activity and religious experiences, Persinger also believes that specific electrical impulses may induce a sense of a "felt" presence, even when there is no one present to evoke such a sense. "This neural phenomenon . . . generates beliefs about supernatural beings and may explain how religious systems originated in the first place" (Schjoedt, 2009, p. 320). Persinger (1983) asserted that "religious and mystical experiences are *normal* consequences of spontaneous biogenic stimulation of temporal lobe structures" (p. 1255). These spontaneous stimulation events are "temporal lobe transients (TLTs)" (p. 1257), which last only a few seconds and may not be accompanied by convulsions, but would still register as anomalous activity in EEG measurements. that's CRAZY!

Persinger and Makarec (1986) designed a self-report inventory to assess complex partial epileptic signs (CPES) in nonepileptic respondents who reported on sensory and perceptual anomalies, visions, ecstatic sensations, and feelings of depersonalization. Higher scores are hypothetically indicative of a higher incidence of temporal lobe transients (TLTs). The authors found "strong correlations between CPES scores and reports of paranormal (mystical, with religious overtones) experiences and 'a sense of presence'" (p. 179). Moreover, higher scores were also associated with suspiciousness, constricted and stereotypical thinking, judgmental thinking, submission to authority, and hypermoralism, which are also characteristic of many epileptic patients. Persinger contends that the unusual or novel sensations and experiences associated with TLTs also involve the amygdala, a part of the limbic system, and therefore suggests that TLTs are a normal brain phenomenon that occur in all people and, since TLTs are also associated with paranormal experiences, may explain the origin of religious belief.

To test his hypothesis that electrical impulses in the temporal lobe could induce religious experiences, including a "felt" presence, Persinger designed the "God Helmet," a modified motorcycle helmet which purports to stimulate the brain through the skull using transcranial magnetic stimulation (TMS) in an effort to induce the experience of an incorporeal but felt presence (Schjoedt, 2009). Participants are not told whether the helmet is active and are instructed to indicate whether they are experiencing a felt presence; results suggest that the God Helmet works on 80% of the general population (Schjoedt, 2009).

Granqvist et al. (2005) have challenged Persinger's findings for several reasons. First, the magnetic fields produced by the helmet are much weaker than ordinary TMS fields typically used in clinical settings to induce brain activity. In fact, Schjoedt (2009) suggests that it is questionable that such extremely weak magnetic fields[1] are capable of "affecting neurons through the skull enough to modulate our subjective experience" (p. 322) and whether there would be an evolutionary advantage for humans to have such sensitivity to such weak magnetic fields. Second, there are unanswered questions about the experimental methods used to get these results. For example, findings from a study by Cook and Persinger (2001) do not address experimental randomization or blindness (the extent to which both participants and experimenters remain blind to whether they are receiving/administering a treatment or a placebo). The third challenge Granqvist et al. address is the extent to which these findings have been replicated independently.

In an attempt to replicate Persinger's findings with greater external validity, Granqvist et al. "attempted to replicate and extend the findings on sensed presence and similar experiences in a controlled, double-blind experimental setting" (2005, p. 2). In addition to seeking to support Persinger's hypotheses that magnetic stimulation of the temporal lobes would result in greater perceptions of a sensed presence, Granqvist et al. also hypothesized that certain personality characteristics like high levels of suggestibility would interact with the magnetic stimulation, making it difficult to interpret which of the two contributed more to the perception of a sensed presence. Upon completion of the replication with an adequate sample size (89 versus 16 for the Cook & Persinger study), experimental randomization, and double-blind administration of the treatment and placebo, Granqvist et al. (2005) reported the following:

> Unlike previous studies in this area we did not find that the application of weak complex magnetic fields caused the sensed presence of a sentient being, mystical or any of the other somatosensory experienced described by Persinger and co-workers. However, personality characteristics indicative of suggestibility consistently predicted the mystical and somatosensory experiences in both religious and nonreligious participants. These characteristics included absorption to mind-altering experiences, the adoption of 'new age' lifestyle orientation, and signs of anomalous temporal lobe activity, which individually explained approximately 10–25% of the outcome variance. (p. 3)

Granqvist and colleagues believe their inability to replicate Persinger's results may have been due to how their experiments differed. While they were careful to maintain a double-blind experimental design where neither experimenter nor participant knew whether they were receiving actual TMS or a placebo, such protocols were not mentioned by Persinger. Granqvist et al. (2005) suggest that "in Persinger and co-workers' studies, highly suggestible individuals may not have been affected by the application of the magnetic fields but may simply have been more prone to pick up on and respond to the experimenter's potentially differential treatments across groups" (p. 5). While Persinger's research has sought to provide empirical evidence for temporal lobe stimulation as the source of religious experiences and sensed presences, the evidence remains elusive. He does, however, have a very interesting helmet.

⌒

Andrew Newberg and Neurotheology

Andrew Newberg has conducted a number of studies and written a number of books and articles that may be summarized under the general heading of *neurotheology*. In the book *Why God Won't Go Away* (Newberg, d'Aquili, & Rause, 2001), the authors offer a summary explanation for their brain imaging research (discussed below) and a neuroscientific defense for the validity of religious and mystical experiences. In his 2010 work *Principles of Neurotheology*, Newberg attempts to provide a systematic set of principles that offer a framework for what he believes to be a new discipline. Newberg describes neurotheology as "a unique field of scholarship and investigation that seeks to understand the relationship specifically between the brain and theology, and more broadly between the mind and religion" (p. 1). While initially based on brain imaging studies related to prayer, meditation, and speaking in tongues, Newberg and his colleagues suggest that this intersection between neurology and theology results from universal brain mechanisms, which have yet to be discovered (Schjoedt, 2009, p. 319). Nonetheless, they offer a view of religion that is both naturalistic and one that views religious experience as "real, authentic, and true" (Day, 2009, p. 116). Newberg has proposed a field of inquiry that is broad and ambitious in its goals, which involve improving our understanding of the mind and brain, religion and theology, and an improvement of the human condition as it relates to health, well-being, and spirituality (Newberg, 2010, p. 18).

One might wonder what neurological findings fostered such a global agenda. Using brain imaging technology, Newberg and his research partner Eugene d'Aquili found that certain religious practices alter an individual's state of consciousness through the increase and decrease of blood flow in specific areas of the brain—specifically the prefrontal cortex, which is involved in higher-order thinking, and the parietal cortex, which is involved in (among other things) providing us with a sense of our spatial boundaries. In one study of eight Tibetan Buddhist monks meditating, Newberg et al. (2001) found an increase in activity in the prefrontal cortex and a decrease in activity in the parietal cortex, which the researchers hypothesized caused the brain processes that separate our sense of self in space from others to suspend, resulting in the experience of *absolute unitary being* (Schjoedt, 2009, p. 315). In a similar study with three Franciscan nuns in meditative prayer, Newberg et al. (2003) found a similar pattern of reduction in activity in the prefrontal cortex and an increase in activity in the parietal cortex.

The activity, or lack thereof, in the parietal cortex is indicative of the function of what Newberg, d'Aquili, and Rause (2001) term the *orientation association area* (OAA). "The primary job of the OAA is to orient the individual in physical space—it keeps track of which end is up, helps us judge angles and distances, and allows us to negotiate safely the dangerous physical landscape around us" (Newberg, d'Aquili, & Rause, 2001, pp. 4–5). The meditation in which the Tibetan monks and Franciscan nuns engaged both showed slowing of activity in the OAA. Without information to process, Newberg and colleagues ask whether the OAA would interpret the lack of boundary information as an indication that such a distinction between self and the outside didn't exist, that "brain would have no choice but to perceive that the self is endless and intimately interwoven with everyone and everything the mind senses. And this perception would feel utterly and unquestionably real" (Newberg, d'Aquili, & Rause, 2001, p. 6). The authors became convinced by the imaging data that these altered states of mind achieved by the monks and nuns were "not the result of emotional mistakes or simple wishful thinking, but were associated instead with a series of observable neurological events. . . . In other words, mystical experience is biologically, observably, and scientifically real" (Newberg, d'Aquili, & Rause, 2001, p. 7).

Another study using brain imaging of five Pentecostal Christians whose worship involves the practice of speaking in tongues (more formally called *glossolalia*) revealed the opposite of the images seen with the Tibetan monks and Franciscan nuns (Schjoedt, 2009). The prefrontal cortex showed a decrease in activity while the parietal cortex showed an increase in activity. "The decrease of prefrontal activity is interpreted as a result of the lack of control during glossolalia which is contrary to the focused attention of meditation" (Schjoedt, 2009, p. 316).

In a review of *Why God Won't Go Away*, Bulkeley (2003) offers two important criticisms of their work. The first is *the lab effect*, which is when "the experimental attempt to replicate a certain kind of experience in a laboratory setting inevitably influences, shapes, and alters the experience in a variety of subtly but significant ways" (Bulkeley, 2003, p. 128), the result being that the experiences to which Newberg and colleagues refer, and upon which they have built the edifice of *neurotheology*, is in fact a unique experience that may not be generalized to similar experiences outside of the laboratory. Bulkeley articulates the distinction this way:

> The question is, are people meditating and praying in a laboratory, "hooked up for electrophysiological readings" as part of a scientific experiment, having the same kind of experience as people meditating and praying in other settings? Newberg and d'Aquili assume the answer is yes, but I would suggest the answer is no. (p. 128)

this is so important

The authors' attempt to "identify a common system of neurological activity responsible for all forms of religious experience" (Bulkeley, 2003, p. 128) leads to Bulkeley's second criticism, namely that the book offers a "runaway universalism" (p. 128). Day (2009) agrees with this criticism, believing that the authors "consistently discount the messy reality of empirical religious heterogeneity in favor of an ecumenical portrait of universal religious homogeneity" (p. 123). In fact, Day is critical of Newberg's methodology, which focuses on neural correlates while ignoring the subjective phenomenological explanations of the experiences accompanying them. While the imaging studies of both the Buddhist monks and Franciscan nuns may have similarities, their self-reported experiences are quite different. The Buddhist monks described experiencing a loss of self and a merging with all creation, while the Franciscan nuns who participated in the study described their experience as a singularly interpersonal connection with God (Newberg, d'Aquili, & Rause, 2001). Day (2009) argues that:

> there is no intelligible way that anyone can legitimately argue that a "no-self" experience of "empty" calm is the same experience as the experience of intense, loving, intimate relationship between two substantial selves, one of whom is conceived as the personal of God of western religion. (p. 123)

[handwritten: everyone experiences things diff]

Satel and Lilienfeld (2013) contend that the limits of neuroimaging are often ignored because of the compelling nature of brain scans.

> Despite well-informed inferences, the greatest challenge of imaging is that it is very difficult for scientists to look at a fiery spot on a brain scan and conclude with certainty what is going on in the mind of the person. . . . One cannot use the physical rules from the cellular level to completely predict activity at the psychological level. (pp. xii, xvi)

[handwritten: scans show what is going on, they don't tell]

A final criticism of neurotheology is offered by Norman and Jeeves (2010), who assert that neurotheology is in danger of becoming a reinvention of a 19th century practice called *phrenology*, which contended that "mental functioning is the result of a discrete number of faculties, each of which corresponds to a separate cerebral organ on the surface of the brain" (p. 235). Inasmuch as phrenology lacked scientific rigor, Norman and Jeeves question "whether investigations of the *relationship* between brain activity and religious/spiritual activity have been scientific" (p. 243). Scientific experimentation often involves the ability to disprove hypotheses; Norman and Jeeves question whether investigations in neurotheology are rigorous enough to either confirm or falsify neurotheological hypotheses. "As was true for phrenology, there is a problem if investigations are designed only to collect confirming evidence or if results are explained in a *post hoc* manner" (2010, p. 244).

Although Newberg's findings are interesting and offer some descriptive value in confirming that the brain is indeed active when people engage in religious experiences, perhaps the enthusiasm to construct a principled system that seeks to integrate neuroscience and theology for the benefit of humankind is a noble, but premature, effort.

⤳

Azari and Distinctive Cognitive Patterns for Religious Experience

Nina P. Azari and her colleagues have contributed three meaningful publications toward the hypothetical relationship between cognition and religious experiences. Her overall research agenda involves the demonstration that, while certain common neural processes are active in religious experiences, there are cognitive processes engaged as well that account for personal and cultural explanations for religious experiences, which necessarily create diverse and even idiosyncratic religious experiences.

In her first study (2001), Azari noted that there are two competing hypotheses for the brain processes engaged in a religious experience. One view is that a religious experience is a "preconceptual, immediate affective event" and would therefore engage those parts of the limbic system which would activate the associated emotions (Azari et al., 2001, p. 1649). The second view, based on attribution theory (a cognitive theory that is concerned with how persons perceive and explain their experiences [Proudfoot & Shaver, 1975]) "would predict brain areas mediating reasoning to be activated" (p. 1649). Azari hypothesized the latter and designed an experiment involving religious recitation that would predict the activation of parts of the brain involved in cognitive mediation.

The study involved six religious and six nonreligious German-speaking adults. The religious participants were all members of the German Free Evangelical Fundamentalist Community, all of whom had reported conversion experiences and believed the Bible to be the word of God. The nonreligious participants were students studying subjects in the natural sciences at the University of Düsseldorf. They were otherwise evenly matched on a variety of other characteristics. Each group was exposed to three stimuli: the first verse of the 23rd Psalm, a popular children's nursery rhyme, and a set of instructions on how to use a phone card. During stimuli exposure, all participants would undergo a PET scan. The religious participants were asked to "induce in themselves and then sustain for the duration of a given scanning session a unique religious state" (Azari et al., 2001, p. 1650). Azari's hypothesis was strongly supported by the results. "The PET images showed a specific, significant activation of the right dorsolateral prefrontal cortex in the religious subjects during the religious state as compared with nonreligious subjects. . . . [The] results strongly support the view that religious experience is a cognitive attributional phenomena" (p. 1651). In addition, Azari did not find activation of the limbic system among the religious participants, suggesting that the religious experience was not an emotional experience. "According to Azari the observation of cortical activities together with the lack of activity in the limbic system, which is normally associated with emotional processing, suggest that religious experience is first and foremost a cognitive phenomenon" (Schjoedt, 2009, p. 323). Further examination of these data (Azari, Missimer, & Seitz, 2005) suggested that a particular neural network was active that involved two forms of expression: the first involved in structures associated with social-relational cognition and also associated with a religious state; the second involved structures associated with "emotion-related language processing, reward, and action preparation" (p. 263). In short, Azari, Missimer, and Seitz (2005) suggest that their findings, along with Newberg's research on Tibetan monks (Newberg et al., 2001), "point to a possible cross-cultural invariance of religious experience, namely an essential relational cognitivity" (p. 275). Hence, all religious experience would necessarily involve the neural processes associated with social-relational cognition.

In their 2004 article, Azari and Birnbacher (2004) revisit the emotion versus cognition debate explored in Azari's experiment with religious and nonreligious participants. Despite the activation of neural processes associated with cognition, Azari and Birnbacher reject the simplistic dichotomy between feeling and thought, concluding that "religious experience emerges as 'thinking that feels like something'" (p. 901). Returning to the attributional theory that provided the theoretical foundation for cognitive involvement in religious experience, Azari and Birnbacher believe that an individual's religious experience must occur within a field of believing, where the belief functions as a framework by which to interpret and evaluate the experience, their relationship to the world, and their conceptualization of God. "The difference between the religious and nonreligious view of the world is not a difference in factual information or factual expectations but in attitudes to the same class of facts" (Azari & Birnbacher, 2004, p. 912).

Social Cognition and Informal Personal Prayer

Uffe Schjoedt (2009) of the University of Aarhus in Denmark conducted a study that used fMRI technology to investigate how different forms of prayer (informal personal prayer, formal prayer, etc.) are associated with specific neural activity in the brain. The purpose of the research was "to describe the basic neural processing employed by religious subjects in various religious practices" (p. 328). Schjoedt divided prayer into two categories: "(a) a highly formalized mode of religion which consists of rigidly performed rituals and prayers and (b) an improvised mode consisting of noninstitutionalized and low-structured practices" (2009, p. 328). Schjoedt hypothesized that improvised petitionary or other forms of conversational prayer would activate the neural substrates associated with social cognition because the participants were conversing with God, who they believed to be alive and capable of a reciprocal response (Schjoedt, 2009). To control for the effects of a formal prayer (the Lord's Prayer), Schjoedt used a well-known nonreligious nursery rhyme. To control for improvised prayer, Schjoedt and colleagues used making wishes to Santa Claus.

The fMRI data supported their hypothesis. When compared with both the nonreligious improvised exercise (wishes to Santa Claus) and religious formal prayer, the areas of the brain that became active while participants were engaged in informal prayer are associated with areas of the brain that are associated with thinking about others' motivations and intentions. Schjoedt contends that this pattern of brain activity during informal prayer more closely resembles talking to a real person (i.e., God) in a normal interpersonal interaction than a fictional person like Santa Claus.

Limitations to the Neuroscientific Study of Religion

One of the important limitations to the neuroscientific study of religion is that the imaging technology permits making correlational hypotheses, not causal hypotheses. To repeat a quotation from the first page of this chapter, "from a scientific perspective, we do not know whether any observed neural activity during a religious experience is the actual cause of the experience, a marker of it, or a consequence" (Mascelko, 2013, p. 205). Moreover, many of the studies lacked *ecological validity*, or the validity to generalize beyond the participants in the study because of the small sample size. A research study may have results that are statistically interesting and meaningful, but those results should not be generalized to a wider population. The findings are specific to that sample.

There were specific methodological problems with the studies cited above. For Persinger's research involving the God Helmet, Granqvist et al. (2005) have challenged Persinger's findings on the basis of the weakness of the magnetic fields used to induce a subjective religious experience, unanswered questions about experimental methods, and a failure for independent replication of Persinger's findings. Granqvist et al. attempted to replicate Persinger's research with greater experimental controls, but found evidence that religious experiences induced by the God Helmet were more likely due to participants' suggestibility.

The research by Newberg and d'Aquili involves small sample sizes for their respective studies: eight Tibetan monks, three Franciscan nuns, and five Pentecostal Christians. A second critique is offered by Bulkeley (2003), who questions the impact of the so-called *lab effect* on participants, which would alter how the brain reacts because of artificial circumstances. The results Newberg and his colleagues found could very well be confounded by the lab setting from which the results were taken. Another criticism voiced by Day (2009) is the assumption of a universal commonality among all religious practitioners, despite the subjective experiences voices by their research participants, which would suggest a very different reality. In similar concern for the scientific basis of neurotheology, Norman and Jeeves (2010) voice a concern that the research has not been scientific. Since scientific experimentation often involves the ability to disprove hypotheses, they are concerned that the investigations in neurotheology aren't conducted in a manner that would provide sufficiently rigorous evidence to support or falsify neurotheological claims. As for the use of neuroimaging in Newberg's research, Satel and Lilienfeld (2013) offer this caution: "one cannot use the physical rules from the cellular level to completely predict activity at the psychological level" (p. xvi).

Azari and her colleagues (2001; 2005) diverge from Persinger and Newberg's hypothesis that "religious experience is mainly a precognitive, primitive, and emotional phenomenon" (Schjoedt, 2009, 322), contending instead that the religious experience is more rooted in social-relational cognition and relies very little on activation of the limbic system, the seat of strong emotions. Methodological issues also involve the small sample size of Christian participants (n = 6) and how the data were statistically analyzed. Schjoedt (2009) notes that statistical significance (a finding that results were unlikely to be due to random error) was not corrected for multiple comparisons; a lack of such statistical correction increases the (often erroneous) probability of believing the results were due to experimental variables and not due to random error.

SUMMARY

- Researchers have found a variety of areas active in the brain when people are engaged in a religious activity or experiencing a religious event. Using various forms of brain imaging technology, researchers have suggested religiosity to be associated with temporal lobe activity (Persinger); prefrontal cortex activation with parietal lobe inactivity or vice-versa, depending on the religious activity (Newberg); brain structures related to social-relational cognition and to "emotion-related language processing, reward, and action preparation" (Azari, Missimer, & Seitz, 2005, p. 263); and the brain areas typically associated with interpersonal relationships and theory of mind activate when believers engage in informal personal prayers (Schjoedt).

- While current brain imaging technology provides much interesting and descriptive information about brain activity during religious experiences, brain imaging is not adequate for making causal relationships. Once again, Satel and Lilienfeld (2013) offer this caution: "one cannot use the physical rules from the cellular level to completely predict activity at the psychological level" (p. xvi).

- Epilepsy, a disease characterized by uncontrollable seizures resulting from dysregulation of electrical activity in the brain, was considered by the ancient Greeks to be "the sacred disease" (Hood, Hill, & Spilka, 2009) because the episodes can be accompanied by changes in perception, hallucinations, and heightened religiosity. Hood et al. note that such an association is "complex, unclear, and generally weak" (p. 62).

- Michael Persinger's research using a "God Helmet" that provided weak magnetic stimulation to the temporal lobe found evidence of religiosity through the reports of a "sensed presence." Granqvist et al. (2005) were unable to replicate Persinger's findings.

- Andrew Newberg and his colleagues use the term *neurotheology* to describe a system "that seeks to understand the relationship specifically between the brain and theology, and more broadly between the mind and religion" (Newberg, 2010, p. 1). Newberg's initial brain imaging research involved scanning the brains of Tibetan monks, Franciscan nuns, and Pentecostals engaged in religious activities, namely meditation for the two former and speaking in tongues for the latter. Notable in their findings was activation of the prefrontal cortex and a lack of activity in the *orientation association area* for those engaged in meditation. The inactivity in the orientation association area suggested a collapse of the boundaries that separate self from the external world, allowing the Tibetan monks to merge with the infinite and the Franciscan nuns to become one with God.

- Nina P. Azari hypothesized that, while there are common neural processes active in all religious experiences, there are specific cognitive processes engaged that are related to social-relational cognition, language processing, reward, and action preparation.

- Uffe Schjoedt (2009) found that informal prayer among Christians was associated with activation of the with "the classic 'theory of mind' areas in social cognition (p. 329), which are associated with thinking about others' motivations and intentions. Schjoedt contends that this pattern of brain activity during informal prayer "suggests that talking to God, who is considered 'real' rather than 'fictitious' like Santa Claus, is comparable to normal interpersonal interaction" (p. 329).

- Limitations of the neuroscientific study of religion include the tentative link between brain imaging at the cellular level and cognition at the psychological level, small sample sizes, methodological difficulties, including designs that lead to an inability to disprove hypotheses.

NOTE

[1] Schjoedt explains these quantitative differences by noting that "while clinical TMS research usually involves fields on the order of 1–2 Tesla to excite brain neurons, Persinger uses magnetic fields measured in nano- and microTesla which approximate the Earth's geomagnetic properties" (p. 322).

3

~~

Making Sense of
Our Perceptions

QUESTIONS TO BE ADDRESSED

1. How do theories of pattern recognition explain our ability to recognize phenomena in our environment?

2. How do these theories relate to the development of beliefs in supernatural beings?

3. What determines how we invest cognitive resources in working memory?

4. How do intuitive, nonreflective thinking and effortful, reflective thinking differ?

5. How do nonreflective and reflective beliefs differ?

6. What cognitive faculties are involved in the categorization of different phenomena?

7. How do we make inferences about phenomena that extend beyond the immediate data we perceive?

8. What expectations do we have of phenomena based on the categories to which they belong?

9. What happens when a phenomenon violates the expectations for the category to which it belongs?

Introduction: Sense-Data and Belief

Belief in religious doctrines and experiences is, directly or indirectly, rooted in trust in the sense-data we perceive in our environment. If we are persuaded by a believer's verbal arguments to adopt their belief, it begins with trust in our auditory faculties and the ability of our brains to make sense of what we hear. If we are persuaded by either something we've seen (e.g., a miracle) or something we've read (e.g., scriptures), it begins with trust in our visual faculties and the ability of our brains to make sense of what we see.

One such example comes from The Book of Mormon, which contains two sections devoted exclusively to statements from witnesses: "Testimony of Three Witnesses" and "Testimony of Eight Witnesses." Both contain statements that the witnesses observed the plates and engravings containing the text given to Joseph Smith by Moroni, "a glorified, resurrected being" (Book of Mormon, vii). The introduction to the Book of Mormon reads:

> In addition to Joseph Smith, the Lord provided for eleven others to see the gold plates for themselves and to be special witnesses of the truth and divinity of the Book of Mormon. Their written testimonies are included herewith as "The Testimony of Three Witnesses" and "The Testimony of Eight Witnesses."

In similar fashion, there are appeals to evidence in the New Testament. The apostle John refers to his own physical encounter with Jesus in the beginning of his first epistle, "What was from the beginning, what we have heard, what we have seen with our eyes, what we have looked at and touched with our hands, concerning the Word of Life . . . what we have seen and heard we proclaim to you also" (1 John 1:1, 3, NASB). The apostle Paul appeals to eyewitness testimony about the resurrection of Jesus. In 1 Cor. 15, Paul writes:

> For I delivered to you as of first importance what I also received, that Christ died for our sins according to the Scriptures, and that He was buried, and that He was raised on the third day according to the Scriptures, and that He appeared to Cephas, then to the twelve. After that He appeared to more than five hundred brethren at one time, most of whom remain until now, but some have fallen asleep; then He appeared to James, then to all the apostles; and last of all, as to one untimely born, He appeared to me also.

Pattern Recognition in Perception

Eyewitness testimony presupposes basic cognitive processes, including perception, attention, working memory, and long-term memory storage and retrieval. The contents of memory are often categorized as semantic or procedural, the former referring to declarative knowledge generally relying on concepts (e.g., water-skiing requires a motorboat or very strong oarsmen) while the latter refers to knowledge related to skills or procedures (e.g., knowing how to pilot a motorboat when someone wants to water-ski).

Since "eyewitness" contains the word "eye," it makes sense to begin with a brief exploration of how visual information is processed. Seeing begins with photoreceptor cells in the retina converting visual electromagnetic energy from a stimulus field into neural signals, which are transmitted via the optic nerve to the primary visual cortex located in the occipital lobe of the brain (Kellogg, 2012). Objects or other phenomena in the stimulus field that generate visual electromagnetic energy are called *distal stimuli*, the retinal images are *proximal stimuli*, and when the images are identified they are referred to as *percepts*.

Identifying percepts involves a cognitive process called *pattern recognition*. It occurs after the conversion of electromagnetic energy generated by the distal stimulus into a retinal image but before the "perception of a stimulus in the environment and its categorization as a meaningful object" (Kellogg, 2012, p. 40). Categorizing the stimulus into a meaningful object involves discernment of its characteristic features and comparing them with information already stored in memory. A match occurs when the pattern of the retinal image is successfully paired with a percept already in long-term memory. Consider the perception of an American stop sign. It has distinct features: an octagonal shape, a red background with a white border, and four white letters that spell the English word meaning "cease movement."

Pattern recognition involves matching all of these features and comparing them with information already stored in long-term memory. Once we retrieve the memory associated with it and make a positive match, we take the appropriate action. Consider how experienced American drivers might respond if the stop sign was triangular, green, or read "HALT." Pattern recognition would be more difficult and the processing time a bit longer.

Cognitive psychologists differentiate between two models of information processing: *bottom-up processing* and *top-down processing*. Bottom-up processing (also called *data-driven processing*) involves the perception of small stimuli in the environment that the brain organizes into something recognizable. When you look out a window, for example, your bottom-up processing will likely see shapes, edges, varying degrees of light and darkness, color, etc., with your brain combining these stimuli into a recognizable pattern (Galotti, 2013). Bottom-up processing begins with the input of a discrete bit of stimulus information into *sensory memory* (the memory process that briefly retains sensory experiences for further processing) and ends with an interpretation based on a match with information in long-term memory (Kellogg, 2012). Posner and Raichle (1994) assert that bottom-up processing is automatic, occurring like a reflex even if the individual is passively engaging with the environment.

Top-down processing (also called *conceptually driven processing*) assumes expectations based on prior learning, reducing "the need to sample all of the information available in the environment" (Kellogg, 2012, p. 43). Unlike bottom-up processing, which begins with perception of discrete stimuli in the environment, top-down processing begins with information already in long-term memory. Existing concepts or mental representations predispose you to experience what you expect to experience. With top-down processing providing a mental model, bottom-up processing detects aspects of that model in the environment, quickly discerning whether the mental model and environmental stimulus match (Kellogg, 2012). "Through such simultaneous processing from both the bottom up and the top down, people can perceive the features of the environment with remarkable quickness and accuracy" (p. 43).

Consider this example. You sit on the porch next to a freshwater lake during the summer, enjoying the sun and cool breeze. As you sit, you see movement in the water that is distinct from the gentle movement of the current in the lake. You immediately detect a long, slender entity moving in a serpentine fashion. The entity has dark edges that are distinct against the lake water. The recognition of all of these sensory stimuli is processed in working memory where top-down processes match the pattern of sight and movement with what you already know about water snakes living in this lake. Soon the harmless snake disappears under the water, leaving the lake surface, dappled with sunlight, as placid as before.

How does this relate to the cognitive psychology of religion? Consider the folklore surrounding the bunyip, a fearsome water spirit of Aboriginal Australia with magical powers. A classic folktale from Robert Holden's book *Bunyips: Australia's Folklore of Fear* (2001) tells of a young man fishing with his companions who captured a bunyip calf. All of the young men knew what their friend had caught and all beseeched him to release it. The calf's cries provoked the enraged mother, who chased the young men in hopes of securing her child. When the fisherman refused to release the calf and even mocked the mother in her distress, she brought desolation to their village, flooding the surrounding land and turning all the villagers into crows. Upon reading this folktale, there are two general hypotheses we might draw. First, the legend surrounding the bunyip began with the same kind of perceptual processes that observed the harmless water snake but grew with the imagination of each teller. Perhaps the fearsomeness of the legend became associated with actual drownings or other water tragedies attributed to unrecognized creatures, growing into the bunyip. Of course, a second hypothesis is that there is indeed a supernatural creature in Australia called a bunyip with powers to call forth the water and transmogrify humans into crows.

There are three commonly suggested bottom-up processing pattern recognition hypotheses: template matching, featural analysis, and prototype matching. Each seeks to explain how we organize sensory data into recognizable patterns.

Template Matching

Template matching hypothesizes that the retinal images (proximal stimuli) we form from our perceptions in the environment is sent to the brain, where the image is compared with existing patterns in long-term memory called *templates* (Anderson, 2010). Recognition occurs when the image is matched with an existing pattern. If there are multiple templates that serve as candidates for a match, further processing occurs in order to identify the match. Such would be the case with similarly-looking letters, like D, B, and P. Templates are similar to stencils—pre-existing patterns that let you trace duplicates of the pattern multiple times. "Templates work like stencils in reverse. An unknown incoming pattern is compared to all of the templates (stencils) on hand and identified by the template that best matches it" (Galotti, 2013, p. 46).

While there may be some element of this type of bottom-up processing, the weaknesses of the template-matching hypothesis are apparent. It assumes we have millions of templates in long-term memory, each matching every possible pattern we could recognize. This would require a significant amount of cognitive processing in the recognition of a single pattern. Moreover, template matching doesn't account for how new templates are stored. Finally, template matching also doesn't account for the recognition of patterns that are recognizable even when the patterns themselves are indistinct, distorted, or fuzzy. Galotti (2013) illustrated this with a simple demonstration. She had 14 people write the same sentence, but the sentences themselves were perceptually different: "You can read each sentence despite the wide variation in the size, shape, orientation, and spacing of the letters" (p. 47).

Featural Analysis

Featural analysis is an alternative to the template matching hypothesis. Rather than relying on matching a distal stimulus with millions of templates, featural analysis reduces the number of representations stored in memory to a small number of geometric shapes that, when combined, encompass all of the potential patterns we might recognize. Biederman (1987) proposed a theory of visual perception involving *recognition-by-components* that is based on the existence of a "modest set of generalized-cone components, called *geons* (N ≤ 36), [that] can be derived from contrasts of five readily detectable properties of edges in a two-dimensional image: curvature, collinearity, symmetry, parallelism, and cotermination" (p. 115). "When these geons are put into proper structural relationships, they constitute all visual objects" (Kellogg, 2012, p. 47). For example, a simple curve and a simple cylinder combine to represent a coffee mug. "An interesting prediction of Biederman's theory is that not only is relational information needed, but it may be more critical to perception than the features themselves" (Kellogg, 2012, p. 48).

While recognition-by-components addresses the storage of millions of mental representations in long-term memory, it fails to address other aspects of perception. For example, how do observers differentiate between objects that share the same geons—a meerkat and a ferret, for example? Moreover, how do observers recognize objects with fuzzy or indistinct boundaries, like clouds or plumes of smoke? These problems in turn suggest the possibility of specific features for different objects. Galotti (2013) summarizes the problem with these questions:

> If there are different sets of features for different objects, how does the perceiver know which ones to use to perceive an object (remember, this must be decided *before* the perceiver know what the object is)? If the same set of features applies to all objects, the list of possible features would appear huge. How then does the perceiver perceive objects so fast? (p. 50)

Prototype Matching

Prototype matching is a perceptual processing theory that addresses some of the weaknesses of template matching and featural analysis. Prototype matching is similar to template matching in that distal images are matched with mental representations in long-term memory. However, the mental representations are not specific templates, but ideal representations of a class of stimuli called *prototypes*. These prototypes serve as exemplars in memory against which distal stimuli are compared. An exact match is not necessary for recognition, permitting a wider range of stimuli to be compared with a smaller number of mental representations. For example, we can recognize variations of the letter G illustrated with different fonts in the box below based on the prototype of the letter G we have in memory. All of the figures below have unique features, but nonetheless match the prototype of the letter G (Galotti, 2013).

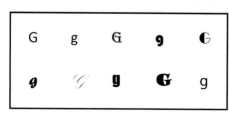

Prototype models allow for more efficient mental processing because, unlike template or featural analysis models, prototypes don't require a stimulus to have one specific feature or set of features. "Instead, the more features a particular object shares with a prototype, the higher the probability of a match. Moreover, prototype models take into account not only an object's features or parts but also the relationships among them" (Galotti, 2013, p. 51).

〜

Attention and Systems of Thought

It is important to note that perceptual processing, whether bottom-up or top-down, occurs rapidly and intuitively. This initial step occurs before the next step in information processing: *attention*. There are multiple hypotheses describing how we attend to certain environmental stimuli. One such theory proposed by Daniel Kahneman (1973) is the *capacity theory* of attention. Unlike so-called *bottleneck theories* that suggest structural limitations in the amount of information that can be filtered, "capacity theory assumes that there is a general limit on man's capacity to perform mental work. . . . A capacity theory is a theory of how one pays attention to objects and to acts" (Kahneman, 1973, p. 8). Kahneman likens paying attention to exerting mental effort, which involves the allocation of cognitive resources available for processing information. These cognitive resources are allocated in *working memory*, which Baddeley (2007) defines as "a limited capacity temporary storage system that underpins complex human thought" (pp. 6–7). Baddeley's definition refers to functions involved in engaging in the mental effort required for a present cognitive task—whether it is trying to remember a name or performing a complex calculation. Each of us has an implicit allocation "policy" that determines how we invest cognitive resources. Among the factors governing this so-called "policy" is the human disposition to attend to novel or threatening stimuli. Such stimuli will automatically provoke the mental effort necessary to process incoming information.

Kahneman (2011) elaborates on his capacity theory of memory by identifying two systems of cognition, which he practically labels as *System 1* and *System 2*. According to Kahneman, "System 1 operates automatically and quickly, with little or no effort and no sense of voluntary control" (2011, p. 20). The processes of pattern recognition occur with System 1 thinking, which is designed to allow us to automatically perceive objects, judge distances, orient ourselves to novel stimuli, make simple calculations, and understand words and simple sentences in our native language. While some of these operations appear to be innate, others are acquired and practiced repeatedly until they become automatic, i.e., little to no cognitive resources must be allocated in order to perform them. Imagine walking home on a moonless night when you suddenly hear what sounds like flapping and an airborne object flies uncomfortably close to you, motivating you to duck. Orienting to the sound of flapping, perceiving the flying object passing close to you, and ducking are all operations derived from System 1.

"System 2 allocates attention to the effortful mental activities that demand it, including complex computations. The operations of System 2 are often associated with the subjective experience of agency, choice, and concentration" (Kahneman, 2011, p. 21). In short, System 2 operations require you to pay attention and may be disrupted by other stimuli that require attention. You may remember back to your elementary school experiences with long division. Doing long division requires attention and concentration, and it can easily be diverted by more interesting things, like video games or paint drying. Kahneman is deliberate when he says System 2 involves paying attention. According to capacity theory of memory, there are a finite amount of cognitive resources available for effortful processing. If we attempt to exceed the resources allotted to the task at hand, it will be unsuccessful. "It is the mark of effortful activities that they interfere with each other, which is why it is difficult or impossible to conduct several at once" (Kahneman, 2011, p. 23).

The relationship between System 1 and System 2 is integral. Kahneman describes "System 1 as effortlessly originating impressions and feelings that are the main sources of the explicit beliefs and deliberate choices of System 2" (Kahneman, 2011, p. 21). System 1 rapidly and intuitively processes stimuli, while System 2 more slowly allows us to better organize those stimuli into orderly thoughts.

∾

From Perception to Knowledge

Both of Kahneman's systems operate with content in long-term memory. More specifically, this involves *semantic memory*, which contains content related to "factual and conceptual knowledge about the world and the words used to symbolize such knowledge" (Kellogg, 2012, p. 314). As the definition demonstrates, *concepts* are important components of semantic knowledge, as are *categories*. Both comprise the "building blocks of human thought and behavior" (Medin, 1989, p. 1469). Medin differentiates between the two as follows: "Roughly, a concept is an idea that includes all that is characteristically associated with it. A category is a partitioning or class to which some assertion or set of assertions might apply" (p. 1469).

Category membership is determined by the degree to which the features of a concept, object, or event are representative of members of that category. The criteria for inclusion or exclusion from a category is probabilistic and is often dependent on the degree of representativeness of a particular example—a robin is more typically associated with the category of "bird" than is an ostrich (Medin, 1989), though certainly both belong in the bird category. The *prototype model* is a good representative of the probabilistic view. Alert readers will remember encountering the term "prototype" earlier in this chapter relating to perception and pattern recognition. Much like its perceptual counterpart, the prototype model allows for categorization on the basis of typicality (called the *typicality effect*). In the prototype model "prototypes of concepts include features or aspects that are characteristic—that is, typical—of members of the category . . . the more characteristic features or aspects an instance has, the more likely it is to be regarded as a member of the category" (Galotti, 2013, p. 171). The prototype model includes Wittgenstein's (1953) notion of the *family resemblance structure* of concepts (cited in Galotti, 2013). As the name suggests, each member of the "family" has several features and shares different features with different members of the family. "Few, if any, features are shared by every single member of the category; however, the more features a member possesses, the more typical it is" (Galotti, 2013, p. 171).

Barrett (2004) identifies several mental tools we use for System 1 thinking, to which he refers as *nonreflective beliefs*, discussed below. "*Categorizers* are mental tools that receive information primarily from our basic senses . . . and use that information to determine what sort of thing or things we have perceived" (Barrett, 2004, p. 4). Categorizers include the faculties that detect faces, objects, and agency, as well as identify animals and artifacts (Barrett, 2004). In terms of the cognitive psychology of religion, the faculty that detects agency, which Barrett calls the *agency detection device*, "looks for evidence of beings (such as people or animals) that not merely respond to their environment but also initiate action on the basis of their own internal states, such as beliefs and desires" (p. 4).

As indicated above, Barrett (2004) describes mental content in memory as beliefs. Believing, like knowing, is a cognitive activity that requires at least the most fundamental form of conceptual organization available for belief formation. Beliefs are not restricted to religion or other value-laden systems; they can be simple like a belief in the trustworthiness of an olfactory sense when smelling bread baking or tacitly demonstrating a belief in a chair's ability to hold oneself by sitting in it. In a fashion similar to Kahneman (2011), Barrett divides beliefs into two broad categories: *reflective beliefs* and *nonreflective beliefs*. Reflective beliefs are roughly analogous to Kahneman's System 2 thinking. Barrett defines reflective beliefs as "those we arrive at through conscious, deliberate contemplation or explicit instruction" (2004, p. 2). Reflective beliefs emerging from cognitive processes involved in reasoning and decision-making are what we more commonly associate with the word "belief," and are often presented in propositional form (Barrett, 2011). Examples include:

1. I believe Blefuscu is a stronger empire than Lilliput.[1]

2. *Gulliver's Travels* is excellent political satire.

3. Hard-boiled eggs are insipid.

Notice that these statements may be true, false, or indeterminate; they can include both statements of fact and opinion (Barrett, 2011). There are concepts and categories embedded in these propositional belief-statements. The phrase "stronger empire" in the first proposition implies both the concept of "empire" and degrees of strength or weakness. The second proposition labels the 1726 novel by Jonathan Swift as "political satire" (generally agreed upon) and describes it as "excellent," a subjective evaluation of quality not necessarily agreed upon. The third proposition is merely a statement of opinion, though use of the word "insipid" is unnecessarily obscure—something only an egghead is likely to use. All three of these propositions, however, are assumed to have resulted from reflective thought.

"Nonreflective beliefs are those that come automatically, require no careful rumination, and seem to arise instantaneously" (Barrett, 2004, p. 2). These beliefs are roughly analogous to Kahneman's System 1 thinking and emerge from the bottom-up pattern recognition processes described above. Nonreflective beliefs may be described as tacit or intuitive, and appear to be produced automatically, requiring very little investment of cognitive resources to form them. Often, we are not consciously aware of our nonreflective beliefs despite the foundational role they play in how we think, speak, and act (Barrett, 2011). Examples of such nonreflective beliefs using the categorizers described above would include our recognition of an apple using the object detection device, or that our dog is an animal and has agency using the animal identifier and agency detection device. Excluding Captain Obvious, rarely does anyone actually articulate these beliefs to someone else (because they are self-evident), but they are believed nonetheless.

Pattern recognition, attention, working memory and knowledge all function adaptively to help us survive. For example, assume you are hiking in the woods and your intuitive belief-producing faculty recognizes a large object partly obscured by a bush. The pattern recognition algorithms in your brain rapidly compare features and patterns to objects in memory. It could be a big log, a mound of dirt, or a sleeping bear. As you draw closer, the object appears to have brown fur. Instantly you discard the log and dirt hypotheses and settle on the belief that it is a bear, because you know bears have fur and logs and dirt mounds don't. Moreover, all of the concepts associated with "bear" become instantly available for conscious action: bears are large, bears are nothing like Smokey or Yogi and are therefore dangerous to humans, bears are strong, bears move fast. Since it appears to be asleep, you may safely and quietly withdraw. Thanks to the cognitive processes we ordinarily take for granted, you have been spared the wrath of an angry bear awakened from its nap.

Application to the Cognitive Psychology of Religion

Boyer's Template and Concept Model

In *Religion Explained* (2001), Pascal Boyer employs a category and concept model similar to what has been described in this chapter. Boyer differentiates between *templates*, which are analogous to Medin's (1989) *categories* and Barrett's (2004) *categorizer* mental tool, and concepts, which are the same as described above. Boyer illustrates this by identifying ANIMAL as a template with specific attributes related to where the animal lives, on what it feeds, how it reproduces, and anatomical features. Concepts that fit into this ANIMAL template include the WALRUS, who lives either in the sea or on the beach, feeds on fish, delivers live cubs, and has a trunk and four legs; and the WOODPECKER, which lives in trees, eats worms and seeds, hatches eggs, and has two legs, wings, and a beak (p. 43).

Boyer (2001) elaborates on the template and concept model by identifying specific operations associated with concept and template matching. *Inferences* are assumptions we make about individual concepts based on the template to which it belongs. In *Through the Looking Glass*, the poem *Jabberwocky* mentions the Jabberwock, with "jaws that bite, the claws that catch" (Carroll, 1897, p. 32). This snippet of information is enough for us to match the Jabberwock with the ANIMAL template, from which we can *infer* that it bears young and has jaws and claws, the former suggesting it to be a carnivore and the latter suggesting a land-dwelling animal. In fact, Boyer contends, these are *default inferences* which we apply intuitively, without reflection (System 1 thinking). Accompanying default inferences are *expectations*. Because we default to certain inferences about the Jabberwock, we would expect it to act in specific ways. We expect it to move on its own power, eat, drink, breed, and eventually die.

Once we perceive and categorize an entity or object, nonreflective default inferences and expectations become operational. These inferences and expectations are embedded in *intuitive ontologies* (Barrett, 2011) which are applied to specific *ontological categories* (*ontology* refers to the essence of being) (Barrett, 2011; Boyer, 2001). Assuming we perceive an object or entity, our pattern recognition processes coupled with knowledge or belief retrieval from long-term memory attempts to classify the object or entity according to our expectations and inferences. According to Barrett (2011), objects or entities may be classified into one or more essential ontological categories: "*Spatial Entities, Solid Objects, Living Things* (that do not appear to move themselves), *Animals,* and *Persons*" (p. 61). These ontological categories correspond to certain essential expectations for each category. The expectation sets are "*Spatiality, Physicality, Biology, Animacy,* and *Mentality*" (Barrett, 2011, p. 61). Each of the expectation sets has essential characteristics associated with objects that fit into these categories.

While ontological categories and expectation sets correspond with one another, they are distinct. Once an entity is perceived and recognized, we intuitively assume specific expectations. The activation of these expectation sets corresponds with one or more ontological categories. The process can be simplified as follows: perception, recognition, expectation(s), and categorization. For example, perception of a large rock intuitively evokes expectations of spatiality (it exists in time and space) and physicality (it is a solid, cohesive entity without independent means of movement). From these expectations we can infer that we would hurt our knee should we strike it. These are characteristic of two ontological categories: spatial entities and solid objects. Table 3.1 summarizes Barrett's description of ontological categories (Barrett, 2011, pp. 61–68).

Barrett (2011) also identifies a set of universal attributes that cut across all of the expectation sets. "They include such assumptions as time moves in one direction, laws and regularities are constant from moment to moment, and causes precede effects" (p. 62). Pyysiäinen (2009) also references intuitive ontology, calling the ontological categories listed above *domains of intuition*. He includes three additional domains: (1) social position, which involves the intuitive assessment of social relationships and hierarchies in groups; (2) events such as actions, rituals, or natural occurrences; and (3) temporarity, which involves the existence of all things in time. The latter would subsume the universal attribute of Barrett's referring to the movement of time in one direction.

Barrett's use of expectation sets and ontological categories provide a framework for understanding how we intuitively perceive environmental stimuli. What, however, happens when something we perceive violates those expectations? When seeing a dog, we apply all the expectations of spatiality, physicality, biology, and animacy. Consider our response should we come upon a dog who is composing a symphony (Barrett & Nyhof, 2001). Since our intuitive expectations for animacy do not include the higher-order mentality for music composition, a dog composing a symphony is considered *counterintuitive* (Barrett &Nyhof, 2001; Barrett, 2004; Barrett, 2011).

Counterintuitive entities are at the heart of religious belief. While no religion we know of is founded on a canine composer (Church of the Musical Mastiff?), many of the beings who populate religious narratives violate expectations of one or more ontological categories. Our expectations for persons do not include the ability to appear and disappear in such a way as to violate the laws of physics, but angelic messengers in numerous religious narratives do so. Consider the birth narrative of Jesus from the second chapter of the Gospel of Luke.

[8] In the same region there were *some* shepherds staying out in the fields and keeping watch over their flock by night. [9] And an angel of

Table 3.1

Expectation Set	Characteristics	Ontological Category	Examples
Spatiality	Location in space and time but lacking in mass	Spatial Entities	Clouds, smoke, shadows
Physicality	Assumes expectation set of spatiality, but includes mass Solidity—occupies a specific location in space that excludes other solid objects from occupying that same space Cohesion—remains a connected whole Inanimate—requires external stimulus to move	Solid Objects	Rocks, bricks, stop signs, hard-boiled eggs
Biology	Assumes expectation sets of spatiality and physicality Growth and development Mortality Reproduction (like produces like) Existence of a "vital force" that powers life	Living Things	Cacti, maple trees, kudzu
Animacy	Assumes expectation sets of spatiality, physicality except for inanimacy, and biology. Goal-directed ability to self-propel, modify appearance (like a chameleon), or make noise Note: self-propelling machines would fit this and lower categories, excluding biology	Animates	Bears, bunyips, dogs, Jabberwocks
Mentality	Assumes expectation sets of spatiality, physicality except for inanimacy, biology, and animacy Presence of consciousness, self-awareness Entities in this category are the object of others' so-called *theory of mind*—intuitive beliefs about what others think, feel, desire, etc.	Persons	Joseph Smith, Lewis Carroll, inhabitants of Blefuscu

the Lord suddenly stood before them, and the glory of the Lord shone around them; and they were terribly frightened.[10] But the angel said to them, "Do not be afraid; for behold, I bring you good news of great joy which will be for all the people; [11] for today in the city of David there has been born for you a Savior, who is Christ the Lord. [12] This *will be* a sign for you: you will find a baby wrapped in cloths and lying in a manger." [13] And suddenly there appeared with the angel a multitude of the heavenly host praising God and saying,[14] "Glory to God in the highest, And on earth peace among men with whom He is pleased." (Luke 2:8–14, NASB)

The use of the word "suddenly" in verse 9 and again in verse 13 indicates the sudden appearance of a single angel and then a multitude of angels. The latter part of verse 9 also tells us something about what happens when our expectation sets are violated—the shepherds were terribly frightened.[2]

Boyer (2001) contends that religious representations (like gods or angels) must meet two conditions: "First, the religious concepts must violate certain expectations from ontological categories. Second, they preserve other expectations" (p. 62). Religious representations—an angel, for example—combine an ontological category (person) and those features that differentiate it from other members of the same ontological category. As mentioned previously, angels preserve many of the expectations of persons but violate expectations related to physicality, where we expect a physical person to remain constant in a space and move in a continuous fashion through space such that we could monitor their movements.

Boyer (2001, p. 63) provides a set of religious concepts that exemplify these conditions using a kind of formula:

Omniscient God [PERSON] + special cognitive powers
Visible ghosts [PERSON] + no material body
Reincarnation [PERSON] + no death + extra body available
Zombies [PERSON] + no cognitive functioning

When we consider these religious representations, we apply the expectation sets analogous to the ontological categories to which the entity on the left side of the equation belongs; in the illustrations above all examples belong to the person ontological category. The right side of the equation contains how that entity violates certain aspects of the ontological category. These violations qualify the entities as *counterintuitive* entities (Barrett, 2011). The concept of counterintuitiveness will be explored in greater depth in the next chapter.

The cognitive faculties we possess allow us to rapidly and intuitively recognize stimuli in our environment using cognitive operations that Kahneman (2011) calls System 1 thinking and Barrett (2011) calls nonreflective thinking. Such pattern recognition processes require us to match environmental stimuli with mental representations stored in long-term memory. Those mental representations include a set of expectations that correspond to the ontological categories to which they belongs. The observation of a bird illustrates the process. We observe an entity with two feet, feathers, and a beak. We organize the stimuli into a recognizable pattern we label "bird." "Bird" is a member of the ANIMAL template and therefore it belongs to the ANIMATE ontological category. We expect it to occupy space, remain cohesive and continuous when moving, be vulnerable to death, and move based on some goal-directed impulse. These are beliefs we assume non-reflectively. Should the bird suddenly begin singing the major-general song from Gilbert and Sullivan's *Pirates of Penzance*, our expectation would be violated and the bird would, no doubt, be the subject of dinner conversation or a doctor-patient interview later on.

SUMMARY

- Many religions appeal to the sense experience of early believers to demonstrate the validity of the associated beliefs.

- Recognition of stimuli in the environment involves two cognitive operations: bottom-up processing and top-down processing. The former is data-driven while the latter is concept-driven.

- Template matching, featural analysis, and prototype matching are bottom-up theories of processing that offer hypotheses for how we recognize patterns in our environment leading to recognition of objects, entities, or events. Theories of speech recognition are analogous to some of the above-described theories of visual perception.

- Kahneman (1973; 2011) theories that we have a limited amount of memory capacity with which to process information. We differentiate between stimuli that require an investment of cognitive resources (i.e., paying attention) and those that may be processed automatically.

- Kahneman (2011) elaborates on his capacity theory of memory by identifying two systems of cognition, which he practically labels as System 1 and System 2. According to Kahneman, "System 1 operates automatically and quickly, with little or no effort and no sense of voluntary control" (2011, p. 20). "System 2 allocates attention to the effortful mental activities that demand it, including complex computations. The operations of System 2 are often associated with the subjective experience of agency, choice, and concentration" (Kahneman, 2011, p. 21).

- Concepts and categories are crucial elements of semantic memory serving as "building blocks of human thought and behavior" (Medin, 1989, p. 1469). Phenomena are assigned to categories intuitively and nonreflectively (System 1 thinking). Barrett identifies specific mental tools that perform these operations, namely *categorizers* and the *agency detection device*, the latter looking for evidence of sentience and the ability to act on the environment independently.

- Barrett's (2011) nonreflective beliefs correspond to Kahneman's (2011) System 1 thinking; Barrett's reflective beliefs correspond to Kahneman's System 2 thinking.

- In *Religion Explained* (2001), Pascal Boyer differentiates between *templates*, which are analogous to Medin's (1989) *categories* and Barrett's (2004) *categorizer* mental tool, and concepts, which are the same as described above. *Inferences* are assumptions we make about individual concepts based on the template to which it belongs.

- According to Barrett (2011), objects or entities may be classified into one or more essential ontological categories: "*Spatial Entities, Solid Objects, Living Things* (that do not appear to move themselves), *Animals,* and *Persons*" (p. 61). These ontological categories correspond to certain essential expectations for each category. The expectation sets are "*Spatiality, Physicality, Biology, Animacy,* and *Mentality*" (Barrett, 2011, p. 61). Each of the expectation sets has essential characteristics associated with objects that fit into these categories.

- Counterintuitive entities, those entities that violate expectation sets associated to the ontological categories to which the entities belong, constitute much of the content of religious belief systems.

NOTES

[1] Fictional island nations appearing in Jonathan Swift's *Gulliver's Travels* (1726).

[2] It should be noted that Christians would contend that it was not only the violation of expectation sets that frightened the shepherds, but also that "the glory of the Lord shone around them." In Christian theology, such epiphanies are almost always traumatic because of the contrast between holy God and sinful human.

4

Cognitive Faculties
and Belief Formation

QUESTIONS TO BE ADDRESSED

1. What faculties enable the human mind to rapidly and intuitively process voluminous amounts of stimulus information from the environment?

2. How do intuitive physics, intuitive biology, and intuitive psychology contribute to our expectations for what we perceive?

3. What cognitive faculties are operative when we perceive mentality and agency in entities we perceive? How do these faculties help us to determine motivation, desire, or intent?

4. What are the advantages in memory and transmission when an agent is perceived as violating one or two expectations for the ontological category to which it belongs?

5. How do supernatural agents benefit from having inferential potential and full-access information to knowledge about moral behavior?

Architecture of the Mind

In the previous chapter we explored the mental systems and processes the mind uses to make sense of what we perceive. Initially, cognitive psychologists viewed "the mind as a 'general-purpose problem-solver' that operated according to a set of procedural rules that could be applied to all forms of information" (Tremlin, 2006, p. 56), including simple pattern recognition. Testing of the general-purpose model soon demonstrated it to be an untenable analogy for the mind, since one set of procedural rules was unable to accommodate to the multiplicity of permutations involved in complex problem-solving (Tremlin, 2006). Many cognitive psychologists believe our ability to process certain kinds of information rapidly and efficiently is due to the *modularity* of our minds (Fodor, 1983). In brief, modularity refers to the existence of multiple mental programs that perform specific tasks, much like Barrett's (2004) *categorizer* tool that allows us to categorize faces, animals, objects, and agents. Another term used to describe modularity is *domain-specificity*, meaning "that a specific brain mechanism is dedicated to processing a specific kind of information (Jeeves & Brown, 2009, p. 60). Facial recognition is one specific demonstration of domain-specificity. Damage to certain parts of the brain can result in a condition where individuals are unable to recognize faces, a condition known as *prosopagnosia*. Kellogg (2012) demonstrates this condition in the case of a sheep farmer who was able to differentiate between photographs of his own sheep and those of other sheep, but is unable to recognize individual human faces. "Faces provide an abundance of social information about an individual's gender, age, familiarity, and emotional state and, in some cases, can allow inferences about the intentions or mental states of others" (Jeeves & Brown, 2009, p. 60). A facial recognition module helps differentiate human from animal, friend from enemy, or friendly versus hostile intent. Moreover, "eyes are one of the first points of contact between infants and their mothers" (Jeeves & Brown, 2009, p. 61).

The contemporary idea of domain-specific modules of cognitive processing may have originated with Jerry Fodor's 1983 monograph *Modularity of Mind*, but similar ideas were expressed about 200 years earlier by the philosopher Thomas Reid (1710–1796), the founder of the Scottish school of common-sense philosophy. Reid articulated a *faculty psychology* that posited the existence of innate mental faculties that permitted the mind to intuitively process information, much like the modularity model of cognitive operations suggested by Fodor. "Reid's 'commonsense' [*sic*] notions of faculties and systematic mental operations are readily explicated in terms of computational and functional analyses being proposed in CCS [computational cognitive science] today" (Smith, 1986, p. 175). For Reid, faculties were the innate, active powers of the mind that functioned in conjunction with one another (Brooks, 1976). Reid categorized the active powers into the mechanical powers of instincts and habits; animal powers of appetite, desire, benevolent and malevolent affections; rational powers involving the transcendent good, morality, and rational anger; and a set of unclassified powers, including attention, deliberation, imitation, and resolution (Brooks, 1976).

Reid's views are noteworthy because they stood in contrast to the predominant view of the associationism of the British Empiricists, who regarded knowledge "as a complex of experiences welded together empirically through the instrumentality of association" (Warren, 1921, p. 9). Rather than through innate mental faculties, British Empiricists like John Locke sought to show "that knowledge arises from experience alone" (Warren, 1921, p. 36).

Fodor's (1983) faculties are input systems, or modules, with very specific functions, much like computer programs designed for a single purpose. For the cognitive processing of visual stimuli, Fodor offers color perception, analysis of shape, and perception of three-dimensionality as sample modules, making them *domain specific* (p. 47). Additionally, modules operate mandatorily, automatically, rapidly, have limited mediation or reflection on input stimuli (i.e., once heard, you can't unhear a sentence), produce shallow (non-conceptual) output, and are *informationally encapsulated* (Fodor, 1983, p. 64), where the action of the modular process is not affected by other processes or feedback mechanisms (Visala, 2011). In fact, Fodor (1983) contends that these modular processes are opaque to other processes: "the output of the perceptual systems is largely insensitive to what the perceiver presumes or desires" (p. 68). The perceptual processes involved with pattern recognition described in the previous chapter would qualify as modules in Fodor's hypothesis.[1] Fodor also argues for the existence of cognitive operations that are not modular. These *central systems* are not domain-specific. Fodor assumes that the input from specific modules must interface somewhere during cognitive processing, "and the computational mechanisms that effect the interface must ipso facto have access to information from more than one cognitive domain" (p. 102).

Others (e.g., Sperber, 1996; Tooby & Cosmides, 1992) have proposed an alternative to Fodor's modularity that is known as the *massive modularity hypothesis*. While Fodor argues for both modular and central cognitive systems that suggests a more limited modularity, those who favor the massive modularity hypothesis argue that almost all human thought processes are modular, that is, computational mechanisms with a very specific set of properties (Eraña, 2012). "The massive modularity model understands the human mind to be a bundle of hundreds, perhaps even thousands, of specialized devices, each applying itself to a single processing demand" (Tremlin, 2006, p. 57). Tremlin offers a list of possible mental modules that include predator detection, food preference, mate selection, childrearing and kinship, and alliance and friendship (pp. 61–62).

The benefit of modularity is the speed with which these automatic cognitive processes process information from our environment, which in turn enables us to react quickly to stimuli we might perceive as threatening. Reacting to a shadow we mistakenly believe to be a fruit bat has the benefit of protecting us, even when we know the shadow won't hurt us. Such rapid cognitive processes allow us to quickly adapt to our environment.

Modularity and Intuition

The intuitive ontologies and expectation sets to which we referred in chapter 3 have corresponding computational modules. These ontological categories correspond to domains described using the premodifiers *folk, intuitive, or naive,* as in *folk physics, intuitive biology,* and *naïve psychology* (Barrett, 2012; Tremlin, 2006; Visala, 2011). These are the automatic assumptions we make about our reality without needing to be taught. Experiments in developmental psychology have demonstrated the presence of intuitive physics by showing that "five-month-olds (and perhaps even younger babies) 'know' that blocks, balls, shoes, and toys have to be contacted in order to start moving, and that when they are contacted by a moving object, they tend to move" (Barrett, 2012, p. 23). A later development for babies during their first year is the knowledge that an object, like a toy or juice cup, must be supported or else it will fall (Barrett, 2012). Babies intuitively know these principles without having to attend classes or lectures in elementary physics, hence the premodifiers *folk, intuitive, or naïve.* For simplicity's sake, I will use the term *intuitive* henceforth.

Tremlin (2006) provides succinct explanations of these important domains, which I will draw from below. *Intuitive physics* "refers to the tacit knowledge about basic mechanical properties and principles that adhere in the world of physical objects, such as solidity, motion, and causality" (p. 67). *Intuitive biology* refers to the intuitive way in which living things are categorized, allowing "a wide range of inferences that apply only to biological organisms, including organic composition, vital functioning, movement, and behavior intentional" (p. 67). We expect manatees to be made of organic substances, not metal or plastic; we expect manatees to give birth to baby manatees; we expect manatees to have a method of locomotion and to move with intention (e.g., finding warmer water). *Intuitive psychology* "refers to the natural attribution of mental states to other people and the cognitive skills involved in the ongoing interpretation of those states" (Tremlin, 2006, p. 68). Perception of stimuli related to these essential domains is governed by the corresponding modules, each with a distinct processing function. For example, Atran (2002) asserts "that there are separate modules that govern interpretation of agency (folk psychology) and essential kindhood (folk biology)" (p. 58).

The key point in understanding modularity is that the processing of information related to these domains occurs involuntarily, reflexively, rapidly, and specific to the domain-related knowledge. For a lesson in intuitive physics, consider the oft-cited passage from Douglas Adams's *Life, the Universe and Everything* (2005), a part of the Hitchhiker's Guide to the Galaxy series. Ford Prefect tells Arthur Dent, "The Guide says there is an art to flying," said Ford, "or rather a knack. The knack lies in learning how to throw yourself at the ground and miss" (p. 75). This bit of tomfoolery is funny (to some) because it obviously violates what we know about intuitive physics. Such efforts would be uniformly met with grass stains or worse should we attempt it on pavement. The module associated with our perception of spatial processing, proprioception, and balance operates without conscious effort on our part; should someone try to help us throw ourselves at the ground, our efforts to right ourselves would occur instantaneously and without reflection.

&

Theory of Mind, Agents, and the Hypersensitive Agency Detection Device

One essential aspect of both intuitive biology and intuitive psychology involves the perception of *agents* and *agency*. Barrett (2004) defines an *agent* as "a being that does not merely respond mechanistically to environmental contingencies but initiates action on the basis of internal, mental states" (p. 125). Barrett's definition corresponds with the expectation sets of two of the ontological categories he describes: *animacy* and *mentality*" (Barrett, 2011). Following Barrett, Pyysiäinen (2009) defines an agent as "an organism to which animacy (liveliness, self-propulsion) and mentality (beliefs and desires) are (correctly or incorrectly) attributed" (p. 12). Atran's (2002) definition of agents emphasizes intentionality and control of self and others. "The central idea is that people, and perhaps other animated objects, are *intentional agents* who act, and cause others to act, on the basis of *internal motivations*" (p. 59). In other words, agents "appear to act on purpose to achieve some preexisting goal; that is, they appear to act *teleologically*" (pp. 59–60). Teleology assumes that there can be implicit, undiscerned reasons why agents act. Our Catahoula Leopard dog Ringo will often vault out of the back door and across the deck with great energy of purpose without ever declaring his intent. He may have seen a squirrel with which he wants to get better acquainted or simply wants to answer nature's call in the great port-o-potty that is our backyard. Though we can't always discern Ringo's reasons for movement, we can be assured that he has a reason.

Entities that we perceive to be animates activate the expectation sets involving spatiality, physicality, and animacy (Barrett, 2011). Examples would include mastiffs, dogfish, alder bark beetles, and American dog ticks. The biology category may also be activated, but mechanical entities like Astro, the robot dog belonging to *The Jetsons*, would also activate spatiality, physicality, and animacy without activating biology (Barrett, 2011). It is also important to note that these may be mistakenly activated such that we attribute spatiality, physicality, and animacy to an entity when in fact it may truly only be spatial and physical (and maybe biological). The branches of a dogwood tree may be waving furiously in the wind, calling to mind the apple-chucking trees of *The Wizard of Oz* or Treebeard and the Ents in *The Lord of the Rings*. However, such attributions would be incorrect in our present reality, since tree branches move because of some external force, not on their own volition.

The expectation set associated with mentality is also activated when the entity we perceive appears to become animate based on some internal motivation and it appears to act on purpose to achieve some pre-determined goal (Atran, 2002). More specifically, when we attribute conscious intention to an organism, we also begin theorizing about its desires and beliefs; we begin a form of mind-reading (Pyysiäinen, 2009). This tendency is a part of intuitive psychology called *theory of mind* (ToM). According to Barrett, "people have conscious mental states that include beliefs, desires (wants), emotions, memories, and percepts. Action is driven by desires and modulated through percepts and beliefs" (2011, p. 75). When we make a mentality attribution to an organism, we assume the existence of a mental state and try to discern or predict that organism's intention. We see a home security salesman walking determinedly up our driveway toward the door. Based on our theory of mind, we predict he is going to try and sell us something, not ask for directions to a garage sale.

Using the language of modularity, the module responsible for perceiving an agent is called the *hypersensitive agency detection device*, or the HADD[2] (Barrett, 2004; 2011). Not only does the HADD determine whether an object is an agent, it also determines "whether some event or trace is the result of agency" (Barrett, 2004, p. 125). Because this device makes agency attributions based on a minimal amount of information, Barrett uses the modifier *hypersensitive*. The hypersensitivity of this device is advantageous because it prepares us to respond to predators or foes. If we detect agency in an object that ends up not being an agent, that *false positive* doesn't have long-term negative consequences. We may think we see a wolf lurking in the bushes, but it ends up being a shadow. No harm done. However, failing to detect agency when the agent has harmful intent does have negative consequences, both short-term and long-term. Short-term, the wolf maims or kills us; long-term, we can no longer pass on our genetic material to offspring, particularly if we're dead.

The tendency toward false positives with the HADD was demonstrated in an experiment by Heider and Simmel (1944). Tremlin (2006) describes the experiment as follows:

> Heider showed adult subjects two-dimensional geometric shapes moving randomly across a flat surface. While these experiments were intended to test thinking about physical causality, subjects also reported their perceptions that the shapes were chasing each other around in space and displaying other intentional behaviors. Because an identifying feature of agents is that they are self-propelled, motion is one of ADD's [HADD's] natural triggers. Subjects went so far as to attribute desires, emotions, and even gender to the shapes. (p. 77)

In addition to the HADD, Pyysiäinen adds two additional agency devices: the *hyperactive understanding of intentionality* (HUI) device, which is the tendency to see events as intentionally caused by some agent even in the absence of the agent's visible presence; and the *hyperactive teleofunctional reasoning* (HTR) device, which is "the tendency to see objects as existing for a purpose" (Pyysiäinen, 2009, p. 13). Taken together, these devices detect agency, intentionality, and teleology, and are the necessary ingredients for activating the expectation set for the ontological category of persons (Barrett, 2011).

One line of research involving the HADD involves theory of mind and autism. Baron-Cohen (1997) asserts the "mind-reading," or the instinctive ways we respond to others in social interaction by anticipating others' desires and motives, is a natural part of human development. "Successful mindreading entails both the ability to think about what others know or believe, and to use this knowledge to generate predictions about how mental states will influence behavior" (Southgate & Vernetti, 2014, p. 1). Moreover, mind-reading is an essential part of the HADD because detection of agency involves making attributions about the agent's desires and motives. Baron-Cohen (1997) asserts that those suffering from autism also suffered from *mindblindness*, a hypothetical inability to discern the underlying mental states of others. An impairment of the capacity for theory of mind may help explain the deficits in communication and social interaction characteristic of individuals with Autism Spectrum Disorder (Scheeren, de Rosnay, Koot, & Begeer, 2013). A psychological experiment involving the *false belief test* conducted by Baron-Cohen, Leslie, and Frith (1983) demonstrates how children with autism differ from typically-developing children. Boyer (2001) provides this explanation for the test involving puppets.

> Puppet 1 puts a marble in box A, and then goes offstage. Puppet 2 arrives on the scene, finds the marble in box A, puts it in box B and goes offstage. Now puppet 1 comes back. The question is: Where will he look if he wants his marble? (p. 103)

Typically-developing children over age four say the puppet will look in box A because that is where the puppet left it. Children three and younger and autistic children say the puppet will look in box B because that is where the marble ended up. Children with autism have difficulty maintaining two mental representations: the false representation in the mind of puppet 1 who thinks the marble is in box A, and the true representation in their own mind that the marble is actually in box B because they witnessed it being placed there (Boyer, 2001). These and other so-called false belief tests provide evidence that autistic children have deficits in the ability to represent other people's representations (Boyer, 2001). As is often the case in the study of the brain, we gain insight into how cognitive operations function by examining processes that appear to be deficient. The social and communicative deficiencies in autism demonstrate the existence of a module commonly called theory of mind. Without a theory of mind, agency detection becomes more difficult.

Before we explore how all of this relates to religion, a summary is in order. The modularity view of the mind sees it as a vast toolbox of specific tools that operate automatically, rapidly, and efficiently to help us adapt to and make sense of our environment. Among the tools are expectation sets for ontological categories into which we place the phenomena we encounter, the most important of these related to agents. As Tremlin (2006) says, "agents can injure and agents can nurture. Agents can attack and agents can protect. Agents can be good to eat and agents can be good at eating" (p. 85). Because of the importance of agents to our survival, the HADD is an essential tool to help us discern which of the above descriptions apply to agents we perceive, or think we perceive. A corresponding tool for employing the HADD is theory of mind. When the HADD determines that the agent is human, theory of mind is an essential part of successful social interaction and building of community. It facilitates empathy, cooperation, enlightened self-interest and, if needed, defense against aggression. Because agency detection is vital to our survival, we frequently detect false positives, that is, we think we've detected an agent when in fact we've detected something that meets some of the expectations of agency—like movement or disembodied vocalization—but in fact is merely an object.

Not only does the HADD equip us to detect agents themselves, but we also detect their traces (Barrett, 2004). We constantly encounter traces of agency in our environment. We detect animal agency when we see a spider's web or smell the remnants of a skunk. We detect human agency when we read books (written by agents), drive cars on roads (both created by agents), etc. According to Pyysiäinen (2009), trace-detection occurs when something triggers the HUI device, leading us to intuitively assume the existence of traces are intentional and designed with some purpose. These intuitive assumptions of agency, intentionality, and purpose involve theory of mind. For example, when we encounter intriguing street art on a wall, the HADD also activates our theory of mind, motivating us to look for intention and purpose in the artwork the street-artist-agent created. This is all pretty routine stuff since we do this daily. Therefore, Barrett (2004) notes that "dealing with known agent traces is the simplest and least interesting way in which HADD handles traces" (p. 37). We find these traces least interesting because they conform to our intuitive expectations. After a certain age, if you've seen one spider web, you've seen them all. However, something quite different occurs when writing appears in the spider's web, as was the basis of E. B. White's *Charlotte's Web*, which is about a literate spider's efforts to save a pig destined for slaughter. A message reading "SOME PIG" appears in the spider web, attracting a lot of attention and garnering publicity for the farm where Wilbur, the pig, lives. Those who were amazed at the event, which should have been all of the humans, not only detected traces of agency, but were unable to account for those traces with ordinary intuitive attributions. The traces in Charlotte's web appear to be purposeful and goal-directed, but more importantly, they do "not appear to be caused by ordinary mechanical or biological causes" (Barrett, 2004, p. 37). The reader knows that those crafty farm animals can communicate with one another and Charlotte (the spider) can write, but the unimaginative people of the community believe it somehow suggests that Wilbur is exceptional and inspires such extraordinary events. In either case, the creatures of the farm are presumed to be violating the expectations associated with their ontological categories.

⤶

Minimally Counterintuitive Agents and Gods

Up to this point, we have talked about our perception of objects and agents as being intuitive. When I see my favorite coffee mug, I intuitively see it as a solid, cohesive object that must be either held or placed on a surface to keep from falling. I can also make inferences about what would happen were I to hurl my coffee mug at the wall. When I see squirrels in our backyard, I see agents that are animate (especially when chased by one of our dogs), maintained by some vital essence, and, by inference, would give birth to little squirrels. When I encounter human agents in the grocery store (I never say "Hello, human agent!"), I know they have emotions, beliefs, and desires. When I see a person frowning and whose brow is furrowed, I have a narrow range of attributions I can make: they can't find the steel-cut oats, they've misplaced their coupons, or the price of sweetened condensed milk has risen dramatically. Given my intuitive theory of mind, I would most likely *not* assume they're happy because kiwis were a dollar per dozen. If the problem was lost coupons, I can infer that I would change their mental state were I to give them my coupons, which I would gladly do because I don't use coupons.

Since our encounters with the objects and agents we see day-to-day can be explained using the ontological categories we've discussed, where does religion fit in? How do we come to develop belief in the supernatural beings that populate religious belief? We develop belief using the same modules we have explored earlier in this chapter. Religious belief "arises because of the natural functioning of completely normal mental tools working in common natural and social contexts" (Barrett, 2004, p. 21). Barrett refers to the broad panoply of supernatural beings as *gods*. Barrett (2004) expands on his definition of *gods* below:

> By "gods," I mean broadly any number of superhuman beings in whose existence at least a single group of people believe and who behave on the basis of these beliefs. Under this definition, I do not discriminate between ghosts, demons, chimeras (such as centaurs or satyrs), or the supreme gods of religions. Even space aliens may

count. They qualify as "gods," for my purposes, as long as people's activity in some way is modified by these beliefs and they are not merely people with ordinary properties of people. (p. 21)

What do all of these "gods" Barrett identifies have in common? The answer is key to understanding both how we develop belief in gods and how such belief is incorporated into a narrative that is widely spread. Gods are *counterintuitive*. Remember that, using modular cognitive processes, we intuitively assign phenomena in our environment into ontological categories. However, ghosts, centaurs, and gods violate one or more expectation sets associated with the ontological category to which they belong (Barrett, 2004; Pyysiäinen, 2009; Tremlin, 2006). In short, "everything that contradicts category-specific, intuitive expectations is counterintuitive" (Pyysiäinen, 2009, p. 26). Something becomes counterintuitive when we intuitively assign it to its proper ontological category, then either an attribute from another category or an attribute from the current category (Pyysiäinen, 2009).

Tremlin (2006) believes that counterintuitiveness is rendered in one of two ways. The first, as mentioned previously, is to violate category expectations. The immortality or omniscience of deities are examples of such violations. The second involves transferring expectations from one category to another. Animals with the ability to reason and speak are examples of transferring expectations from the PERSON category to the ANIMAL category. While immortality and omniscience don't belong to any ontological category and are therefore purely violations, transferring is also a violation of our expectations.

Boyer (2001) uses a helpful formula that demonstrates how agents can be counterintuitive. Ghosts, for example, are described as follows:

Ghosts [PERSON] + no material body

When Ebenezer Scrooge first saw Marley's ghost in Charles Dickens' *A Christmas Carol*, he immediately recognized him as the person Jacob Marley. Ghosts are associated most closely with the PERSON ontological category, which also subsumes the lower ontological categories of spatiality, physicality, biology, and mentality. However, because ghosts are transparent and can walk through solid objects, they violate expectations associated with the PERSON category. The above illustration reflects Pyysiäinen's (2009) notion of subtraction in that the ghost is a person without corporeality. This is also an example of transferring ontological expectations from the SPATIALITY category, which involves characteristics associated with smoke and shadows, to the PERSON category.

If you imagined that my favorite coffee mug could discern my thoughts and say "You look like you could use some coffee," the formula would be as follows:

Coffee Mug [OBJECT] + mentality (thought, speech)

The coffee mug violates the ontological category of OBJECT by transferring attributes associated with PERSON.

Violations of expectation sets associated with ontological categories force us to become reflective, requiring us to increase the amount of attention we devote to the counterintuitive phenomenon. In effect, counterintuitive phenomena shift our thinking from Kahneman's System 1 to System 2, which "allocates attention to the effortful mental activities that demand it, . . . the subjective experience of agency, choice, and concentration" (Kahneman, 2011, p. 21). Attention devoted to counterintuitive phenomena requires more cognitive effort, and therefore increases the probability of memory encoding and retrieval. Tyler, Hertel, McCallum and Ellis (1979) conducted experiments to demonstrate that high-effort cognitive tasks would lead to better recall than low-effort cognitive tasks. Participants were given anagrams to unscramble and sentences to complete at both low-effort and high-effort levels. Low-effort tasks were easy to complete, while high-level tasks were more difficult. "For example, the word *doctor* was transformed into anagrams *dortoc* (low effort) and *croodt* (high effort)" (Tyler et al., 1979, p. 609). After completing the tasks, participants were given a surprise word-recall quiz. The authors found that significantly more high-effort words were recalled (18.6%) than low-effort words (11.1%). Research by Barrett and Nyhof (2001) exposed participants to narratives involving both intuitive (e.g., an earthworm), and counterintuitive items (e.g., a carrot that talks). They found that counterintuitive items were more easily remembered than intuitive items. The significance of these and other studies relates to how well a concept is remembered *and culturally transmitted*. Successful religious concepts are those that are easily understood, remembered, and transmitted to others. One important characteristic of memorability is *counterintuitiveness*. Religious concepts that involve agents who have characteristics or attributes that are unexpected are more easily remembered. The novelty of these attributes increases the salience of concept; you are more likely to remember a fish who told you a story than a fish who gaped at you from behind the glass of its fishbowl.

It is important to note that there are degrees of counterintuitiveness. Some of the items in the Barrett and Nyhof (2001) research (e.g., talking carrot) are considered *minimally counterintuitive*. Barrett defines *minimally counterintuitive* as:

> concepts that match up with the intuitive properties of a sort of thing but include a small number of violations of expectations. Though the number of violations is not precisely known, it seems that one or two in any one context serve as a limit. Being minimally counterintuitive endows a concept with a greater likelihood of being remembered and faithfully transmitted. (2004, p. 126)

In the same Barrett and Nyhof (2001) research referenced above, they also experimented with a story about a person visiting a museum containing 18 exhibits that could be classified into three categories: counterintuitive, bizarre, or common. Counterintuitive items were those that "possessed a feature that violates intuitive assumptions for the object's category membership (e.g., a living thing that never dies violates assumptions about all living things)" (Barrett & Nyhof, 2001, p. 78). Bizarre items had highly unusually characteristics but didn't violate category-level assumptions, like a dog weighing over 11,000 pounds. While it is highly unusual for a dog to weigh that much, it doesn't violate expectations for living things in general (Barrett & Nyhof, 2001). Items in the common category contain neither category violations nor bizarre features; they would be classified as intuitive. After three generations of retelling, results indicated that counterintuitive items were remembered significantly better than bizarre items, which were remembered significantly better than common items. The authors also found that 37.5% of the bizarre items were distorted in retelling to be counterintuitive items. Why were these items more easily transmitted and recalled? "Counterintuitive concepts were simply more memorable, and unusual properties tended to be changed into counterintuitives" (Barrett & Nyhof, 2001, p. 83)

Degrees of counterintuitiveness imply an optimal number of violations for memorability and ease of transmission. For example, Atran (2002) differentiates between minimally counterintuitive and maximally counterintuitive concepts, which would contain a higher number of category violations. Think about the folktales or myths with which you are most familiar. Rarely do they contain maximally counterintuitive agents. Consider any of our commonly-told folktales. We have talking animals, but we don't have talking animals that are immortal, turn into wisps of smoke on Thursdays, and can foretell the near-future (Barrett, 2004).

Barrett, Burdett, and Porter (2009) examined 73 folktales from around the world for degrees of counterintuitiveness using a coding scheme proposed by Barrett (2008), with one goal being to "provide evidence concerning just how counterintuitive is too counterintuitive for a concept to be a recurrent cultural idea" (Barrett et al., 2009, p. 271). The table below exemplifies counterintuitive ideas from Barrett et al.'s study

Table 4.1

Counterintuitive Idea	Counterintuitiveness Score
A horse that talks	1
A dead woman who comes back to life	1
A talking tiger that gives birth to domestic cats	2
A dead woman who comes back to life only at night	2
A dead woman who comes back to life and takes off her head only at night	3

(Adapted from Barrett, Burdett, and Porter, 2009, p. 289.)

with a corresponding score ranking the ideas' counterintuitiveness. Higher scores indicate more violations of expectations. Barrett, Burdett, and Porter (2009) found that "the cognitive optimum for cultural transmission falls around one counterintuitive feature" (p. 271).

Other research supports the hypothesis of the memorability of minimally counterintuitive concepts. Boyer and Ramble (2001) conducted a number of experiments similar to those conducted by Barrett and Nyhof (2001) in cross-cultural settings. Their "results supported the hypothesis that violations (either *breaches* of relevant expectations for a domain or *transfers* of expectations from one domain to another) produce a retrieval advantage" (Boyer & Ramble, 2001, p. 557). More significantly, Boyer and Ramble suggest that limited, or minimal, violations are optimal for recall. Upala, Gonce, Tweney, and Slone (2007) conducted research that supported the recall advantages of minimally counterintuitive concepts but also added that memorability also involves "the context in which the concept is presented, and the background knowledge that the comprehendor possesses about the concept" (p. 433).

Boyer (2001) and Boyer and Ramble (2001) use the device of metamorphoses as an example of the optimal advantage of minimally counterintuitive concepts for recall. Moreover, metamorphoses in myths and folktales "illustrate how supernatural imagination is more structured than we would usually assume" (Boyer, 2001, p. 67). Drawing on the work of Ovid and the Brothers Grimm, Kelly and Keil (1985) found that these storytellers told tales populated with counterintuitive agents whose counterintuitiveness revealed conformity to specific properties of conceptual structure.

> Ovid and his fellow mythmakers and story tellers certainly did not create metamorphoses with the purpose of mirroring conceptual structure. Rather, they constructed tales in order to fulfill some social goal, such as edification and entertainment of citizens, socialization of children, and veneration (or, in Ovid's case, possibly depravation) of the gods. Any metamorphoses portrayed in stories were designed to advance these other goals. (p. 404)

Kelly and Keil (1985) found that metamorphoses generally occurred between ontological categories that were closer together. "Persons are turned into animals more often than into plants, and into mammals and birds more often than insects and bacteria; animals are turned into other animals or plants more often than inert natural objects" (Boyer, 2001, p. 67). The proximity of the ontological categories associated with the changes is more optimal for recall than changes involving distant categories. As Boyer notes, "persons and animals are seldom turned into artifacts" (2001, p. 67).

To provide a proper context to the application of religion, let us consider an essay written in the 17th century by the Scottish clergyman Robert Kirk entitled *The Secret Commonwealth*. The subtitle of the essay reveals its purpose, which was to describe the nature and actions of the so-called subterranean people, otherwise known as elves, fauns, and fairies. Moreover, Kirk seeks to demonstrate the compatibility between Christianity and the fairy stories of pre-Christian paganism. The essay records the stories told to him by his parishioners of those with "second sight" who had encounters with the "good people" of the supernatural world. One explanation for belief in fairies is that they were the indigenous people, the Picts, who ruled Scotland before being vanquished by the Danes and later the Anglo-Saxons. Defeated, "the Picts had literally gone underground, and lived in their fairy forts hidden from view of their successors, but audible—on occasion—from the sounds of their hammerings in their tunnels" (Kirk, 2007, p. xxi). The reverend Kirk wrote to contradict this naturalistic explanation, asserting that "fairies exist alongside humans on the one hand, and God and his angels (and the devil and his) on the other, and that they inhabit a parallel universe which disconcertingly impinges and intermingles with men and women" (Kirk, 2007, p. xxi).

The reverend Kirk's description of "the good people" is a case study in counterintuitiveness. They are

> intelligent studious spirits, and light, changeable bodies (like those called astral) somewhat of the nature of a condensed cloud and best seen in twilight. These bodies be so pliable through the subtlety of the spirits that agitate them that they can make them appear or disappear at pleasure. (2007, p. 6)

He goes on to describe that "their chameleon-like bodies swim in the air" as they restlessly change their lodgings quarterly and walk abroad, and those with second sight "have very terrifying encounters with them, even on the highways" (2007, p. 7).

Consider how such a description of fairies might prime the HADD to detect agency. Fairies fit the ontological category of PERSON but violate the expectations of corporeality, being able to appear and disappear. Given the cultural context, it would be natural for a rural traveler to believe they had encountered fairies as they walked abroad. Kirk recounts the story of "a minister, very intelligent but misbelieving all such sights as were not ordinary" (2007, p. 28) walking along a narrow lane with one with second sight, a seer. The seer perceives a wight whom he recognizes aggressively coming toward them and he encourages the minister to get out of the way. The minister, seeing nothing, refused, with the result that "they were both violently cast aside to a good distance, and the fall made them lame all their life" (p. 29). Soon after the minister was carried home, "one came to toll the bell for the death of the man whose representation met them in the narrow path some half an hour before" (p. 29).

After reading Kirk's account and recalling that the HADD often renders both true and false positives, we may infer at least two hypotheses. The first is that the minister and seer encountered something natural on the road that violently tossed them aside, and the seer, remembering the activation of his HADD and theory of mind, and drawing upon his knowledge of the ways of the fairy, (wittingly or unwittingly) reconstructed the event to recall the wight. The second hypothesis is that the minister and seer did encounter a supernatural agent with violent intent and suffered their injuries as a result.

In his essay *On Fairy-Stories*, J. R. R. Tolkien wrote, "The mind that thought of *light, heavy, grey, yellow, still, swift*, also conceived of magic that would make heavy things light and able to fly, turn grey lead into yellow gold, and the still rock into swift water" (Tolkien, 2008, pp. 335–336). Fairy tales, folktales, myths, and religious stories share common elements that make them memorable: events or entities that do not behave as we expect them to behave. As Tolkien (2008) puts it, they have an "arresting strangeness" (p. 262). Although we may compare religious stories with fairy tales and myths on the basis of what makes them memorable, there is no assumption that all such stories are fiction. In fact, it may be argued that fairy tales, folktales, and myths are themselves religious stories, containing information about the transcendent and the mysterious. In his essay *Myth Became Fact*, C. S. Lewis (1970) illustrates this:

> In the enjoyment of a great myth we come nearest to experiencing as a concrete what can otherwise be understood only as an abstraction. . . . What flows into you from the myth is not truth but reality . . . and therefore, every myth becomes the father of innumerable truths on the abstract level. (p. 66)

Lewis himself embodied this understanding of the intersection of myth and belief in his description of his own conversion to Christianity to his friend Arthur Greeves:

> Now the story of Christ is simply a true myth: a myth working on us in the same way as the others, but with this tremendous difference that it really happened: and one must be content to accept it in the same way, remembering that it is God's myth where the others are men's myths: i.e. the Pagan stories are God expressing Himself through the minds of poets, using such images as He found there, while Christianity is God expressing Himself through what we call "real things." (Hooper, 1996, p. 569)

The Kalapalo people of central Brazil also demonstrate how myth and reality intersect. The Kalapalo mythology is populated with powerful beings, first people called Dawn People, a classification of various beings by the sounds they make, and rituals highly dependent on music. For the Kalapalo:

Strange behavior on the part of an individual can be likened to some action of a powerful being in a myth, and so interpreted. An eclipse of the sun or moon recalls stories in which the sun or moon are "being killed," but also reassures in that in the stories they do not die, but return to their normal state. . . . Myth is an account of the way things are, a reference frame for understanding the world. (Bellah, 2011, p. 142)

～

Inferential Potential and Intuitive Morality

We have already established that minimally counterintuitive agents increase the probability of memory and transmission. However, not all minimally counterintuitive agents are interesting enough to be transmitted at all, much less retained and transmitted as *religious* concepts. For Barrett (2004), successful MCIs are those that are salient in memory and therefore the likeliest to spread. "Though an invisible tree is just as much an MCI as a listening tree, ethnographers tell us that things like trees and rocks that listen appear much more commonly in belief systems" (p. 25). One reason for this difference is because the listening tree is a *supernatural agent* associated with the PERSON category. "Religious concepts are those supernatural concepts because of the attributes that *matter*. The world over, people entertain concepts of beings with special qualities and special powers" (Boyer, 2001, p. 137).

Related to supernatural agency is *inferential potential*, particularly as it relates to making sense of highly relevant phenomena, like the success or failure of crops, whether the river will flood its banks, how to ensure the fertility of livestock, or making sense of death. MCIs that have the greatest likelihood for cultural transmission are those that "have the potential to explain, to predict, or to generate interesting stories surrounding them" (Barrett, 2004, p. 25). MCIs with inferential potential also activate other cognitive tools, such as those described by Pyysiäinen (2009) as the hyperactive understanding of intentionality (HUI) device and the hyperactive teleofunctional reasoning (HTR) device. Additionally, MCIs have the potential to activate a group of cognitive tools Barrett (2004) calls *facilitators*, which concern themselves with intuitive social regulation. Tools concerned with religious concepts include the social exchange regulator, social status monitor, and an intuitive morality tool.

For supernatural agents to matter significantly to a religious belief system, they are typically involved in regulating moral matters. Barrett (2004) contradicts the assumption that morality is culture-bound and relative.

Contrary to what many believe, religions do not invent morality wholesale and insert gods as the final arbiters over right and wrong. Rather, people the world over seem to have massively overlapping senses of what constitutes moral behavior. This regularity across cultures casts grave doubt on the alleged arbitrariness or relativity of morality. (p. 47)

Intuitive morality is a tool that helps to regulate social interaction. Without moral guidelines, communities would lapse into chaos, losing the benefits otherwise gained by forming a community. How do gods and religion relate? Boyer's (2001) explanation is that gods, spirits, and ancestors are *"interested parties* in moral choices and moral judgments, rather than providers of codes and rules" (p. 189). Because they are supernatural agents, they are often assumed to have what Boyer calls *full-access information* related to our behavior and whether it is right or wrong; supernatural agents know everything they need to know about a situation or event to adjudicate its morality. Boyer refers to this type of information as *strategic information* (p. 189). Strategic information is information that we assume the supernatural agent has that allows for full adjudication of a given behavior: motives, intent, and outcome whether it was retribution for a wrong done, an act of altruism, or a blatant violation of the moral code. The activation of our theory of mind (ToM) also suggests that we assume that the supernatural agent has the same moral intuitive as we do (Boyer, 2001).

It is important for our adaptation and survival to use the same strategic information, though limited by our lack of omniscience, to regulate our social interactions in such a way that we maximize our access to the resources that allow us to survive (Barrett, 2004). As such, when we attribute knowledge of strategic information to supernatural agents, we also attribute the power to act, either to punish for disobedience or reward for obedience. "By having full access to a dispute with moral considerations, a god would know who is in the right and could mete our justice or sympathize with those who have been wronged" (Barrett, 2004, p. 50). Such attributions also contribute to our understanding of misfortune and death and inform the importance of ritual in religious observance (Visala, 2011). The Old Testament figure of Job illustrates the application of intuitive morality and full-access information. After the calamity of losing his children, wealth, and health, Job's three friends Eliphaz, Blidad, and Zohar came to sympathize with and comfort him (Job 2: 11–13). Throughout the narrative, the comfort his friends provide consists of maintaining that God is punishing Job for some transgression, bringing such dire misfortune on himself. Eliphaz persists in this explanation throughout the narrative, at first gently admonishing one who had been such help to others ("Your words have helped the tottering to stand, And you have strengthened feeble knees," Job 4:4) to the seeming hysterical charge that Job had oppressed the widow and the orphan ("You have sent widows away empty, And the strength of the orphans has been crushed," Job 22:9). Job protests his innocence to the point of calling God to account for what has befallen him. We know from the first chapter of Job that his suffering came at the hands of the Adversary Satan, not because of Job's own transgressions. Nonetheless, his three friends were unable to conceive of any other explanation for Job's misfortune.

Pyysiäinen (2004) suggests that supernatural agents with full-access information are also helpful in decision-making. Decisions of life-and-death or fortune and misfortune are best undertaken when we are capable of consulting the agent who knows. Barrett (2004) offers an example described by anthropologist Scott Atran to illustrate the explanatory power of supernatural agents and fortune or misfortune. A Mayan hunter was bitten by a dangerously venomous snake and refused any kind of Western medical care. Instead, he listened to the forest spirits, whom he expected to tell him which plants to use to save his life. "After consulting the forest spirits, he gathered a few choice plants, applied them, and fully recovered from the bite" (Barrett, 2004, p. 55). Given the context of the hunter's belief in the forest spirits, it was entirely consistent for him to consult them and follow their advice for the remedy. This exercise of belief also reinforces the belief, strengthening the inferential and explanatory power of the belief system. As Barrett (2004) explains,

> Each time we satisfactorily understand an episode as being the work of a god, another memory is created affirming the existence of the god, and the mental tools responsible for such problem solving have more tightly woven the existence of the god into its operating assumptions. (p. 55)

Putting It Together

All humans are endowed with cognitive faculties that rapidly and intuitively process information from our environment. Once we recognize the pattern of a stimulus and are able to put a semantic definition to it, we also intuitively classify it based on the ontological category to which we believe it belongs. We also have a set of expectations that we attribute to the stimulus, based on the properties of its ontological category. We expect spatial and physical objects, like clouds and rocks, to be subject to our assumptions about intuitive physics. We expect plants and animals to be subject to our assumptions about intuitive biology, as well as intuitive physics. We expect people to be subject to our assumptions about intuitive psychology, which we approach using an aspect of intuitive psychology called theory of mind, which includes assumptions of agency, and intentionality. Part of the cognitive tools we use in service of intuitive psychology is the hypersensitive agency detection device, which is highly sensitive to changes in our environment and alerts us to the presence of agents and/or their traces. Because of its hypersensitivity, we are prone to false positives.

When we perceive something in our environment that violates one or more of the expectations we associated with an ontological category, this gets our attention. The novelty of this counterintuitive experience increases our attention and makes memory of the experience easier to retain. Minimally counterintuitive concepts, those who violate only one or two expectations from their ontological category, are often easiest to remember. If we perceive agency in these minimally counterintuitive stimuli, this activates our theory of mind and tools associated with social interaction and regulation. If this is a supernatural agent, the agent must have full-access to strategic information related to moral behavior. We recognize the power differential and the importance of maintaining the good graces of the supernatural agent who knows our thoughts and behaviors. We perform certain rituals to gain the favor of this supernatural agent or perform rituals to atone for moral failures. When these rituals are followed by positive outcomes, the behavior and belief system is reinforced.

The contents of *The Secret Commonwealth* and the common belief in fairies in Ireland and Scotland illustrate how these cognitive faculties coordinate to form a belief system based on the subterranean people. A highlander is abroad after dark and is crossing a lake. Being mindful of the stories he's heard around his turf fire about the little people, his HADD is on full alert. While on the lake, he sees unusual lights under the water some distance away. He believes he hears the sounds of merry-making, and assumes he's come close to one of the underwater fairy-forts. He knows they are aware of his presence (because they are super-natural agents) and the potential for mischief should he ignore them, so he takes one of the loaves of bread he was bringing home for his family and throws it into the lake, thereby acknowledging them and giving an offering to them. He continues on undisturbed, further convinced of the existence of fairies and the importance of offerings to them to ward off their mischief.

SUMMARY

- The architecture of the mind is conceived as having modules that perform rapid, nonreflective tasks, like categorization of faces, animals, objects, and people. Fodor believed in the presence of modules that were domain-specific but also a central processor that coordinates modular information. Others have suggested a massive modularity model, which "understands the human mind to be a bundle of hundreds, perhaps even thousands, of specialized devices, each applying itself to a single processing demand" (Tremlin, 2006, p. 57). The key point in understanding modularity is that the processing of information related to these domains occurs involuntarily, reflexively, rapidly, and specific to the domain-related knowledge.

- Modules related to ontological categories create expectations for entities to observe rules associated with intuitive physics, intuitive biology, and intuitive psychology.

- One essential aspect of both intuitive biology and intuitive psychology involves the perception of *agents* and *agency*. Barrett (2004) defines an agent as "a being that does not merely respond mechanistically to environmental contingencies but initiates action on the basis of internal, mental states" (p. 125).

- The module responsible for perceiving an agent is called the *hypersensitive agency detection device*, or the HADD (Barrett, 2004; 2011). Not only does the HADD determine whether an object is an agent, it also determines "whether some event or trace is the result of agency" (Barrett, 2004, p. 125). Because this device makes agency attributions based on a minimal amount of information, Barrett uses the modifier *hypersensitive*.

- When we encounter violations of ontological categories, or counterintuitive concepts, we are forced to invest more cognitive resources in order to attend to the novelty. Those which are the best candidates for memory and transmission are those who only possess a minimal amount of violations of their ontological category.

- Minimally counterintuitive entities that we perceive as having agency are often perceived as being supernatural, or as Barrett (2004) defines them, gods.

- "Religious concepts are those supernatural concepts that *matter*. The world over, people entertain concepts of beings with special qualities and special powers" (Boyer, 2001, p. 137).

- Supernatural agents, or gods, have inferential potential because they "have the potential to explain, to predict, or to generate interesting stories surrounding them" (Barrett, 2004, p. 25).

- Supernatural agents operate within the same intuitive morality as we do and have full-access knowledge about the extent to which we conform or fail to conform to that morality. Misfortune is explained as the consequence of moral failure, while fortune is explained as the result of moral excellence.

Notes

[1] While Fodor's modules have similar characteristics to Kahneman's System 1 thinking, the latter involves the use of biases and heuristics to make judgments and form conclusions, the process of which would appear to violate some of Fodor's criteria for modules, including informational encapsulation and shallow output (Prinz, 2006).

[2] The terms "hyperactive" and "hypersensitive" are used interchangeably.

5

Childhood Development and Cognitive Faculties for Belief

Questions to Be Addressed

1. How does cognitive development as hypothesized by Piaget relate to how children think about religion?
2. How do other developmental models correlate with Piaget's model of cognitive development?
3. What empirical evidence exists for innate religiosity in early childhood?
4. What are the three hypotheses for how children learn about God?
5. What empirical evidence exists for innate morality and its relationship to religion in early childhood?

A Child's Theology

One of my childhood memories involves a seven-year-old me discussing the attributes of God with my neighborhood friends. A girl insisted God was everywhere, and I thought that must mean He had to be in her long brown hair. In my mind's eye, I had the image of God somehow curled up like the Cheshire cat on her head. At that point, I had had no formal religious training, but accepted without question my friend's theology. Later I would learn that this bit of folk theology was formally referred to as God's omnipresence. Around the same time, I was introduced to the first ghost story that truly terrified me. While waiting in line at school, I overhead other students saying, "Don't you dare say Mary Worth ten times in the mirror!" I learned that to do so would invite the ghost of Mary Worth to appear and kill whoever summoned her. There were dead children, my friends claimed, to prove this. Being only a second-grader, I accepted this supernatural story as true and went home beside myself with fear. In a misguided attempt to help me, my parents brought me into the bathroom to show me it wasn't true. They only got to three Mary Worths before my panic convinced them this was not the best idea. I had been told that there were no such thing as ghosts, but to my seven-year-old mind their existence was as plausible as God's existence, since both inhabited the unseen but nonetheless real world of the supernatural.

The psychiatrist Robert Coles wrote a book entitled *The Spiritual Life of Children* (1990), where he records conversations of children from all faith traditions and includes a selection of their drawings representing depictions from their various faith traditions. Coles writes of a conversation he had with twelve-year-old Asif, a devout Muslim who wanted to be a pilot. His rationale was that he wanted to be closer to Allah. Asif said,

> I don't know if it would be right—but I'd say my prayers on the plane, and He might hear them better up there. It must be hard for Him, when all of us pray to him [in the mosque]. I asked my father, and he said not to worry, Allah hears every word. But it might help if I was nearer—higher up toward where He is. (Coles, 1990, p. 226)

Asif also told Coles that God would make things better on a plane should it encounter trouble. He said,

> Our God wants us to obey His laws, and if a pilot is praying to Him, then the plane is safer. . . . If you pray to Him, you'll be stronger; you will be purer, and you will be a better pilot. If you don't think of Him, and don't pray, you will be weak, and you could make mistakes. (Coles, 1990, p. 227)

Embedded in these narratives is an understanding of the attributes of supernatural agents, from ghosts to an all-powerful God. How do these beliefs develop?

Developmental Models

Piaget and Cognitive Development

Since this is a book about the cognitive psychology of religion, we should begin with Jean Piaget (1896–1980).[1] His observations of children led Piaget to hypothesize that children progress through four stages of cognitive development: sensorimotor, preoperational, operational, and formal. The *sensorimotor stage* spans birth to 18–24 months. Piaget believed the infant did not have the capacity for mental representation at this stage, so knowledge was acquired through sensory and motor experiences (Galotti, 2013). One important milestone that occurs during the sensorimotor stage is the development of *object permanence*. When younger infants become interested in a novel stimulus (e.g., a toy) but soon see it obscured, they lose interest. Older infants will continue to search for the toy despite it being obscured. Piaget suggested that this change indicates that the infant's initial response of losing interest demonstrates their lack of ability to retain mental representations. Older infants (8–12 months) will continue to search for the toy after it has been obscured, indicating that they have acquired the ability to retain mental representations (Galotti, 2013). During this period, infants begin building knowledge associated with space, time, and causality. "Infants experiment, draw causal connections, invent means-ends procedures and frequently give indications of insight" (Fowler, 1980, p. 54).

The *preoperational stage* roughly spans ages 2–7. During this stage children develop the ability to engage in symbolic functioning: "pretending to drink from an empty cup, cradling a doll or stuffed toy as if it were a baby, 'riding' on a 'pretend horse' made of a stick" (Galotti, 2013, p. 325). Similarly, children's symbolic functioning enables them to develop language to describe their experiences; language allows for children to identify, remember, and talk about their experiences, actions, and feelings with others, activating language as a socialization tool (Fowler, 1980). Children during the preoperational stage have difficulty sustaining the perspectives of others, making them *egocentric*. Egocentrism in preoperational children simply means that the child's perspective predominates their thinking, making it very difficult to simultaneously maintain their own and another's perspective. For example, a child observing a phenomenon will assume others can see the same details of the phenomenon, even if others do not have the same vantage point as they do. For example, a preoperational child describing the zoo to his grandmother on a cell phone will assume Grandma can see the same monkeys, even if the monkeys are in Atlanta and Grandma is in Grand Rapids. Piaget and Inhelder (1967) conducted an experiment where preoperational children were shown a miniature model of three mountains with different items in the foreground on each side and a wooden doll on the opposite side of the child. When they were asked what they thought the doll saw, they reported that the doll could see everything the child could see, failing to account for their different positions (cited in Galotti, 2013).

Another important aspect of the preoperational stage involves the important role of perception. While children are capable of maintaining mental pictures of what they perceive, they have difficulty testing the inferences they make based on their perceptions and therefore have a poor understanding of causal relations (Fowler, 1980). "The child's feelings and fanciful imagination have free rein to fill in the gaps in understanding that perception leaves" (Fowler, 1980, p. 57), which often manifests as magical thinking.

Concrete operations spans ages 7–12 and involves the introduction of a form of logical thinking in the child. "The operational logic of childhood gives rise to a construction of reality that is increasingly orderly, predictable, and temporarily linear" (Fowler, 1980, p. 64). This enables the child to engage in the classification of objects or items based on their characteristics with much greater ease than the preoperational child. Finally, the onset of concrete operations permits the child to maintain multiple perspectives, diluting the egocentrism that is characteristic of the preoperational stage. Piaget described this kind of thinking as *decentered* (Galotti, 2013).

The fourth and final stage of cognitive development is the *formal operations stage*, which begins in early adolescence. This stage is characterized by more abstract thought and the ability to imagine more possibilities beyond that which the empirically-oriented concrete child imagines (Galotti, 2013). "For concrete thinking . . . *possibility* is a subset of *reality*; for formal thinking . . . *reality* is a subset of *possibility*" (Fowler, 1980, p. 71). Reflection is another characteristic of formal operations, allowing for *meta-cognition*, or thinking about thinking; "the adolescent begins to be able to reflect on the life course from 'above' or 'beside' it" (Fowler, 1980, p. 71).

Ernest Harms and the Development of Religious Experience in Children

Scholars interested in religious development have used Piaget's cognitive developmental model as a framework for understanding how children develop religious beliefs. Interestingly, one scholar, Ernest Harms, appears to have anticipated some of Piaget's findings with his 1944 article *The Development of Religious Experience in Children*. Harms's experiment began with a diverse sample of school children of all ages being asked to imagine how God would look to them; adolescents and post-adolescents were also given the option of presenting "the meaning of religion as such and of the highest ideal expressed in religion" (Harms, 1944, p. 114). Analysis of the results yielded Harms to hypothesize the existence of three stages of religious experience: the fairy-tale stage, the realistic stage, and the individualistic stage.

Harms and his colleagues collected and analyzed about 800 drawings from children ages 3–6 and concluded that most of the pictures had the common characteristic of illustrating their version of God in fairy-tale form. Regardless of the illustration, "the formal language in which this deistic experience was expressed was always that of the fairy tale. For this is the form in which the child of this age-group experiences the major portion of his mental life" (Harms, 1944, p. 115). Harms also noted a distinct difference between the child's experience of God and other fairy-tale experiences, namely that of a sense of reverence and awe for the being to whom the child directs her religious attention. Harms deems this a noteworthy observation, "since it seems to point to the fact that children have a leaning toward a God experience from the time their consciousness awakens" (p. 115).

The realistic stage of religious experience is characterized by a realism that avoids the child's formerly fantastic conception of God. As part of their socialization, children are introduced to church teachings, often presented in organized forms like catechisms. Harms's analysis of the drawings of these children revealed a fascination with symbols. The Crucifix and Jewish Star were common symbolic representations of God. When children chose to represent divinity through people, they were no longer fairy-tale representations but ethical elements expressed as "human figures, helping, assisting, influencing human life and supervising man's ways on earth" (Harms, 1944, p. 117).

For the third stage of religious individualism, Harms and his colleagues examined around 4000 pictures of adolescents and post-adolescents. They divided the pictures into three groups: groups A, B, and C. Group A consisted of individuals who expressed their religious representation in a conventional way in accordance with their own religious tradition. Group B consisted of individuals whose expression of their religious experience emphasized their inner world and their independence from the traditional religious notions associated with their parents' religion. The drawings in this second group were noteworthy for keen emotional sensitivity, originality, and inventiveness (Harms, 1944). Group C contained representations that were remarkable for being "far removed from the patterns of the child's original environment. Furthermore, they could not have been introduced from any religious outside source" (Harms, 1944, p. 119). These pictures contained elements of ancient Egyptian cults, Persian mythology, Chinese Buddhism, Celtic sun worship, alchemy, Indian Mandala meditation, Rosicrucian mysticism, and pantheism.

> The most fascinating drawing of the entire group, however, was one deifying the medical profession. The picture portrayed a landscape; in the skies above, the giant figure of a doctor was drawn, and in the foreground a mass of people were crowded, raising their arms in distress. The picture bore the inscription "Doctor Help." This fourteen-year-old child's deistic conception was the idea of medicine, personified by the doctor who watches over the well-being of the world. (p. 119)

Hopefully it will be easy to connect Harms's stages with Piaget's stages of cognitive development. Harms's fairy-tale stage with deities depicted as figures from fairy tales or myths is consistent with Piaget's preoperational stage, where imagination and emotion yield magical thinking. Harms's realistic stage with an emphasis on symbols and institutional religion reflects Piaget's concrete operational stage with the ability to classify and organize mental representations. Harms's individualistic stage with its idiosyncratic depictions of religious imagery and symbolism is consistent with the abstract reasoning found in Piaget's formal operations stage. While Piaget's method was more systematic and thorough than the analysis of the drawings of school children, Harms's work appears to converge with Piaget's.

David Elkind: Children, Cognitive Need Capacities, and Religious Development

David Elkind (1970) offers a theory of the origins of religion in children that begins with the assumption of the accuracy of Piaget's stage theory of cognitive development. The progression through the cognitive stages of development with increasingly elaborate mental abilities also creates *cognitive need capacities*. The development of the cognitive capacities that enhance thinking also create tension between the child and her environment. Elkind (1970) offers two examples. When the child acquires a basic understanding of cause-and-effect, she begins asking "why" questions. She finds "that parents do not appreciate such questions, particularly when they are endlessly repeated. The child's attempts to realize his capacity for causal understanding thus bring him into conflict with the adult world" (Elkind, 1970, p. 36). Secondly, once a child develops a facility for quantitative relations, concerns for fairness and equity make the distribution of crackers an exact science. "In short, every cognitive capacity is in itself a need which prompts behaviors that can create discord between the child and his social and physical milieu" (Elkind, 1970, p. 36).

In concert with Piaget's four stages of cognitive development, Elkind (1970) identifies four cognitive need capacities: conservation, representation, relation, and comprehension. Each of these, Elkind contends, are addressed by the four major elements of institutional religion: the God concept, Scripture, worship, and theology. The sensorimotor stage ultimately creates the capacity for object permanence, or conservation. "Infancy thus bears witness to a new mental ability, the capacity to deal with absent objects, and to a corresponding need, *the search for conservation,* a life-long quest for permanence amidst a world of change" (Elkind, 1970, p. 37). As the child develops into adolescence, this capacity for conservation comes into conflict with the inevitability of death. They appear to be irreconcilable. However, the problem appears to be solved in God, who embodies conservation by transcending space, time, and physicality. "By accepting God, the young person participates in his immortality and hence resolves the problem of the conservation of life" (Elkind, 1970, p. 38).

The preoperational stage introduces the use of language and symbolic communication. As such, it also involves the cognitive need of *representation.* Like conservation, Elkind notes that the need for representation that appears during the preoperational stage remains a need throughout life. As we grow and learn, we strive to represent the contents of our inner life and external environment with increasing accuracy. "Yet, the more exacting the child becomes in his search for representation, the more dissatisfied he becomes with the result" (Elkind, 1970, p. 38). The child realizes that language is a clumsy means for expressing thoughts and is wholly insufficient for expressing emotion (Elkind, 1970). This would be truly problematic with the acceptance of God as a means to resolve the conservation need without a way to represent a God concept through language. This need for representation is resolved in how the corresponding religion represents God. For world religions like Christianity and Islam, there are scriptures that are revered and believed to communicate the Word of God. For local or tribal religions, such symbolism is often expressed in idols or other objects often called *totems* that represent the religion.

Piaget's operational stage corresponds with the beginning of formal education and involves the ability to reason with logic, leading the child to try to make sense out of her world by relating phenomena systematically (Elkind, 1970). "It seems appropriate, therefore, to speak of the new ability that surfaces at school age as *the capacity for practical reason* and of the corresponding need as *the search for relations*" (Elkind, 1970, p. 39). The acquisition of this ability continues throughout life as we all attempt to make sense out of the things that happen. Sometimes our efforts at understanding the relatedness of things are successful, but sometimes the effort is fruitless. As mentioned in the previous chapter, the Old Testament story of Job not only includes the concept of intuitive morality, it also demonstrates the very human tendency to search for relations that explain tragedies that befall. Job's friends insisted these disasters were related to Job's own sinfulness, while Job in his agony was unable to relate what had befallen him to anything.

Elkind contends that this tendency for relatedness is addressed in religious belief. "Religion, however, affords a means whereby the individual can relate himself to the deity, for it offers the sacrament of worship. By participating in worship, the young person can relate himself to the Transcendent in a direct and personal way" (Elkind, 1970, p. 40). Religious expressions of relatedness to God serve other functions as well. They strengthen the beliefs of those who practice them and encourage the spread of those beliefs to others (Barrett, 2004).

The formal operations that appear during adolescence enable the capacity for abstract thought and development of theories that underlie the relations among elements identified earlier in childhood. According to Elkind (1970), the need capacity associated with this development is *comprehension*. Like the previous need capacities, comprehension is only partly successful in helping us make sense of the world. "In modern religions, the resolution to the problem of comprehension is provided by theology" (Elkind, 1970, p. 41). This need capacity is addressed in many religions through the codification of doctrine into confessions, catechisms, and definitive works of theology. Judaism not only has the Old Testament, but also the Talmud, the rabbinic commentary on the Old Testament. Protestant Christianity not only has the New Testament, but the Westminster and Belgic Confessions that seek to encapsulate the doctrines of Protestantism. Many world religions have catechisms, concise summaries of the major tenets of their respective faiths.

Elkind is not willing to say that all religion exists merely as a response to these four cognitive need capacities.

> The concept of God, Spirit, or more generally, the Transcendent, cannot be reduced to the search for conservation any more than it can be traced to the phenomenon of death. Contrariwise, neither the search for conservation nor the phenomenon of death is in itself religious, although it may well take part in the production of religious elements. Like a Gestalt, such as a painting or a melody, the Transcendent is greater than the sum or product of its parts. (Elkind, 1970, p. 41)

James Fowler and the Stages of Faith

James Fowler (1980) offers a stage theory of faith development that incorporates not only Piaget's cognitive development model, but moral and psychosocial models of development as well. Fowler was intentional in identifying these as stages of *faith*, as opposed to religion or belief. Fowler draws heavily from the work of Wilfred Cantwell Smith and his book *The Meaning and End of Religion* (1963). Smith differentiates between faith and religion. He defines religion as being the summary of cumulative traditions, while "faith, at once deeper and more personal than religion, is the person's or group's way of responding to transcendent value and power as perceived and grasped through the forms of cumulate religion. Faith and religion . . . are reciprocal" (Fowler, 1980, p. 9). For Fowler, faith is a human universal that embodies the human relationship with the transcendent. Faith is not a single dimension of a multidimensional life, but "an orientation of the total person, giving purpose and goal to one's hopes and strivings, thoughts and actions" (Fowler, 1980, p. 14).

Fowler identified seven stages of faith. The first is *undifferentiated faith* of infancy, which Fowler labels as a pre-stage. During this developmental period, the infant's earliest experiences are building a foundation for the nature and quality of her faith experience. The infant's interactions with her primary caregiver(s) help develop a sense of mutuality and trust as needs are met and, as the infant's primary narcissism gives way to the recognition of the existence of others, a rudimentary form of reciprocity develops. Abuse or neglect at this stage makes the infant's environment untrustworthy and dangerous, encouraging them into isolation and fear of relationships. Such conditions do not provide fertile ground for the growth of healthy faith.

The onset of language and symbolic communication leads the infant into the first stage of faith, the *intuitive-projective* stage, which, like Piaget's stage, spans ages 3–7. Though capable of thought, the child at this stage has not yet learned to bridle her thought with the logic that is characteristic of later years. As such, religious images and symbols combine with the child's emotions and imagination to produce highly salient and emotionally evocative images that strongly affect the child's subsequent faith development. "Imagination in this stage is extremely productive of long-lasting images and feelings (positive and negative) that later, more stable and self-reflective valuing and thinking will have to order and sort out" (Fowler, 1980, p. 133).

The *mythic-literal faith* of the second stage is characterized by cognitive operations that are orderly, logical, and empirical. The fantastic images of the intuitive-projective stage are now subject to more careful examination. Moreover, while the child in the intuitive-projective stage of faith is characterized by episodic images, the mythic-literal child has developed "a more linear, narrative construction of coherence and meaning. Story becomes the major way of giving unity and value to experience" (Fowler, 1980, p. 149). Moreover, Fowler contends that children at this stage accept a literal interpretation of the tenets of their faith community and expect reciprocal fairness to govern events and relationships.

Fowler entitles the third stage *synthetic-conventional faith*. Because this faith stage corresponds with the onset of formal operations, "there is a reliance on abstract ideas of formal operational thinking, which engenders a hunger for a more personal relationship with God" (Hood, Hill, & Spilka, 2009, p. 84). Although associated with adolescence, many adults remain in this stage throughout their lives (Fowler, 1980). Because the onset of adolescence involves the management of multiple domains—family, peers, school, work, church—"faith must synthesize values and information, it must provide a basis for identity and outlook" (Fowler, 1980, p. 172). In addition, Fowler also argues that this stage is characterized by conformity to the expectations of significant others within the faith tradition, and, while loyally and deeply held, tenets of the faith tradition are not critically or independently examined such that the individual "owns" their faith.

In Fowler's (1980) paradigm, the movement from stage three to stage four offers opportunity for a crisis of faith. Confronted with the necessity of taking responsibility for their beliefs and behaviors, the individual at this stage is negotiating the following tensions:

> Individuality versus being defined by a group or group membership; subjectivity and the power of one's strongly felt but unexamined feelings versus objectivity and the requirement of critical reflection; self-fulfillment or self-actualization as a primary concern versus service to and being for others; the question of being committed to the relative versus the struggle with the possibility of an absolute. (p. 182)

The result of resolving these tensions are resolved in stage four, *individuative-reflective* faith, which produces a greater reliance on self-as-authority rather than the external authority of others, the ability to examine deeply-felt commitments critically, and a greater sense of commitment to convictions consciously chosen (Hood, Hill, & Spilka, 2009).

The fifth and sixth stages, *conjunctive faith* and *universalizing faith*, appear to depart from a purely developmental paradigm into a more phenomenal model that deals more directly with immediate experience. According to Fowler, *conjunctive faith* involves an acknowledgement and embrace of ambiguity and the recognition of truths that transcend specific ideological and religious boundaries. During this stage, the individual embraces a kind of dialectic that "is open to the multiple perspectives of a complex world" (Hood, Hill, & Spilka, 2009, p. 84). *Universalizing faith* is rare and "involves a oneness with the power of being or God, as well as commitment to love, justice, and overcoming oppression and violence" (Hood, Hill, & Spilka, 2009, p. 84).

Some criticisms of Fowler's stages of faith model have focused on his attempt to integrate multiple developmental progression models into a single model without accounting for incompatible differences between models (Jardine & Viljoen, 1992). For example, in Piaget's model, the next stage of operations cannot be attained until the previous stage has been adequately mastered. Conversely, embedded in Fowler's stages of faith are elements of Erikson's (1963) psychosocial development model, where progression occurs inevitably through biological maturation, regardless of how well the particular tasks of the psychosocial stage have been negotiated. This makes the uniform progression through the stages of faith unlikely at best, increasing the potential for fragmented development. Another problem raised by attempting to integrate multiple models for distinct domains is noted by Smith (1977), who "points out that because Fowler combines the work of various theorists, the reader no longer knows which details have been empirically validated and which have not" (Jardine & Viljoen, 1992, p. 74). As final concern is that Fowler's progression through the faith stages is contingent on cognitive development. Consequently, many adults "run the risk of being relegated to an adolescent category . . . on the grounds of their being characterized by concrete-operational thinking" (Jardine & Viljoen, 1992, p. 80).

Streib's Religious Styles Model

Heinz Streib (2001) offers an alternate conceptualization to Fowler's stage approach. Streib believes a stage theory relies too heavily on cognitive development to the exclusion of other important aspects of religion, including its content, function in the individual's life, and the experiences the shape the individual's perceptions of religion. Streib also believes that a privileging of cognition as the "motor of religious development" (p. 144) neglects other seminal relationships: self-self, self-Other, self-tradition, and self-social world. Streib proposes replacing stages with religious *styles*, which places "more emphasis on the factors of life history and life world for religious development" (p. 146). Finally, Streib associates the developmental framework Fowler uses, with its "structural, hierarchical, sequential, and irreversible logic of development" (p. 155) with the so-called *modernity project*, which itself is overly optimistic about providing a satisfactory explanation for developmental phenomena. Such an approach fails to account for the postmodern challenges that require a more interpersonal and nuanced approach to religious narratives. Streib's styles provide for the necessary changes to those narratives that authentic encounters with the Other often precipitate.

While Streib's (2001) styles roughly correspond with Fowler's stages, they are unlike stages because they do not follow a hierarchical structure nor have the invariant sequencing of a stage approach. Instead, an important aspect of development involves "working on and coping with the integration of previous styles" (p. 149), suggesting a more fluid and overlapping movement among the styles. Streib's *subjective religious style* developmentally corresponds with Fowler's (1980) intuitive-projective faith. The subjective religious style develops as a result of the young child's relationship experiences, providing a foundation for the development of a God representation which continues as part of the subsequent styles. A child that conceives of a punitive God will likely integrate that into subsequent manifestations of religious belief and practice. This is how styles differ from stages. For Fowler, the intuitive-projective faith stage gives way to the mythic-literal faith stage, but Streib's subjective religious styles integrate into the subsequent religious styles that emerge as part of the individual's faith development.

Streib's (2001) *instrumental-reciprocal style* corresponds with Fowler's (1980) mythic-literal faith stage. This style is characterized by an emerging sense of differences between the intrapersonal, or inner self, and interpersonal, or outer self. The *instrumental* aspect of this style refers to the child's awareness of and pursuit of her own needs and interests, while the *reciprocal* aspect of this style establishes the relational pattern "both for the interpersonal and the God-human relationship: 'Good' is what God and the authority persons wish and demand; 'bad' is what results in punishment and mischief; means of trade are obedience and fulfillment of religious commandments" (Streib, 2001, p. 151). In addition to the establishment of these relational patterns, religious imagery and emotions become part of the dominant religious narrative. At this age, the narrative is wholly literal, without an understanding of any symbolic elements that may be present. "Literally everything happened precisely as told in the story; literally everything has to be observed exactly as the religious rules prescribe" (Streib, 2001, p. 151).

Streib's (2001) *mutual religious style* emerges with the expansion of the child's interpersonal experiences and "rests on the mutuality of relationships in one's religious group and prefers an image of God as a personal partner" (p. 152). The cohesiveness of the religious group and the security it provides makes transcending the group difficult. Though Streib does not specifically relate this to Fowler's (1980) synthetic-conventional faith, the importance of the group is an important component of both. Streib's fourth style, the *individuative-systemic style*, which corresponds to Fowler's *individuative-reflective faith* stage, is characterized by an openness to reflect on religious beliefs and traditions and the ability to offer a defense for the reasons for belief. Conversely, religious texts and rituals "are deprived of their symbolic quality and reduced to propositional statements" (Streib, 2001, p. 152).

Streib's (2001) final style is the *dialogical religious* style. Like Fowler's (1980) conjunctive faith stage, this style is characterized by a greater openness to other ideas and traditions, where contradictions do not necessarily lead to exclusion. "When we are no longer predominantly concerned with finding and defending our own religious identity, we are able to open up to and learn from other people with religious orientations different from our own" (Streib, 2001, p. 152).

Although each developmental theory has its distinctions, all involve cognitive operations that emerge with increasing sophistication in understanding and practicing religion. The table below provides a comparative summary of the theories mentioned above.

Table 5.1   Religious Development Theories Compared

Age	Piaget	Harms	Elkind	Fowler	Streib
Infancy	Sensorimotor		Conservation	Undifferentiated	
3–7	Preoperational	Fairy tale	Representation	Intuitive-projective	Subjective religious
7–12	Concrete operations	Realistic	Relation	Mythic-literal	Instrumental-reciprocal
Adolescence	Formal operations	Individualistic	Comprehension	Synthetic-conventional	Mutual religious
Early adulthood				Individuative-reflective	Individuative-systemic
Mature adulthood				Conjunctive, universalizing	Dialogical religious

Evidence of Innate Religiosity in Early Childhood

A number of research studies with infants and children suggest the presence of cognitive modules dedicated to mental operations associated with naive religion. You may remember earlier exploring mental modularity (Fodor, 1983) as an explanation for how we process information rapidly and intuitively. The thoughts, emotions, and behaviors that emerge are the natural consequences of modular processing. In fact, these natural consequences are the inevitable result of normal development and occur automatically, easily, and fluidly (Barrett, 2012). McCauley (2011) called these kinds of automatic processes *maturational naturalness*. "Learning to walk is maturationally natural. Understanding that you have to touch a solid object to make it move (as in picking up a coffee cup) is maturationally natural" (Barrett, 2012, p. 17). These and other early developmental milestones are differentiated from later actions that *become* natural through repeated practice, like writing or bike riding (McCauley, 2011). Though they eventually become automatic, McCauley calls this kind of cognitive processing *practiced naturalness*. McCauley (2011) identifies four criteria for an action or behavior to be maturationally natural:

1. It must occur early enough in childhood such that it isn't recalled (remember learning to chew?).
2. It isn't associated with an artifact or tool, like a crayon or bicycle.
3. It doesn't require a practiced mentor or guide to facilitate learning.
4. It isn't specifically culturally mediated, meaning it should occur regardless of the culture.

Barrett (2012) contends that there are several maturationally natural cognitive processes that constitute the foundation of religious thinking, including *teleological functioning,* or the belief that natural entities exist for a purpose; *intelligent design attribution* (Kelemen & DiYanni, 2005), or the belief that *someone* rather than *something* or *nothing* is responsible for creating natural things like birds or lemons; and the superhuman agency of God, or the belief that God functions superhumanly regarding perception and omniscience, moral judgment, and immortality. Barrett (2012) summarizes empirical research studies that support the notion that infants are naive theists in his book *Born Believers: The Science of Children's Religious Belief*. Some of these studies with their respective authors are discussed below.

Pyysiäinen (2009) hypothesized that we possess a *hyperactive teleofunctional reasoning* (HTR) device, which is "the tendency to see objects as existing for a purpose" (p. 13). Developmental psychologist Deborah Kelemen and her colleagues conducted several experiments with children at varying ages exploring teleological functioning. Kelemen et al. found an overwhelming tendency among children to believe that living and nonliving natural phenomena exist for a purpose (Kelemen, Casler, Callanan, & Pérez-Granados, 2005). She referred to this as *promiscuous teleology*—"*teleology* meaning that children find design and purpose in the world, *promiscuous* in the sense that they find purpose with very little evidence and in places that adults might find inappropriate" (Barrett, 2012, p. 46). Kelemen contends that this is the default explanatory style of children, as opposed to *selective teleology*, which suggests that teleological explanations are restricted to biological entities and their parts; nonliving artifacts like rocks, mountain peaks, and rivers would be excluded (Kelemen, 1999).

Kelemen (1999) explored promiscuous teleology by asking four- to five-year-old children to choose who was right: Ben or Jane. One argued that items on a list including living things, biological parts of living things, natural object parts (e.g., cloud parts), artifacts, and artifact parts were all made for something; the other argued against that. For example, children were shown a picture of a tiger and pictures of Ben and Jane. They are then told, "Point to who you think is right. Ben who thinks a tiger is made for something or Jane who thinks that's silly because a tiger isn't made for anything" (Kelemen, 1999, p. 256). After being presented with all of the objects, 75% of children's responses favored the person making the teleologically functional argument.

In another set of experiments, Kelemen (1999) explored the tendency among both adults and children to explain the properties of both living and nonliving things in teleological terms, with the hypothesis that the younger the child the more likely they were to reveal a promiscuous teleological tendency. Both children and adults were asked whether the properties of animals and rocks were designed for a purpose, e.g., why are rocks pointy? In contrast to the adults, "children at all grade levels promiscuously viewed the properties of nonliving natural objects as existing for a purpose. In other words, children in all grades . . . preferred teleological over physical explanations of the properties of objects such as rocks and stones" (Kelemen, 1999, p. 1445). These findings did not extend to adults. Kelemen concluded that her research suggests that promiscuous teleology remains intact until mediated by formal scientific education.

As we explored previously, *agency detection* is a vital cognitive operation that enables us to respond rapidly to threats or opportunities, predators, or prey. This is the role of the *hypersensitive agency detection device* (HADD). Often, the HADD is activated when we detect *traces* of agency, like graffiti or crop circles. Kelemen and DiYanni (2005) asked British elementary school children questions about the origins of both living and nonliving things. Children were asked both open-ended and closed-ended questions about laminated photographs of artifacts (hat, boat), animals (bird, monkey), natural events (thunderstorm, flood) and two nonliving natural objects (mountain, river). The children were first asked the question "Why did the first ever X exist/occur?" where X refers to the items in the photographs. After being asked these open-ended questions, they were asked two sets of questions with options to select. The first set asked that they choose from a physical explanation of the origin of the item (e.g., "'The first ever thunderstorm occurred because some cold and warm air all rubbed together in the clouds') and a teleofunctional explanation of origins (e.g., 'The first ever thunderstorm occurred to give the earth water so everything would grow')" (Kelemen & DiYanni, 2005, p. 11). The second set were the so-called *intelligent design* questions, where children were asked questions like, "'So we've been talking about mountains. Now here's the question. Did someone or something make the first ever mountain exist or did it just happen?'" (Kelemen & DiYanni, 2005, p. 12). The question offered children three choices: someone (intelligent design), something (a nonintelligent cause), or spontaneous generation.

The results for the teleofunctional versus physical explanations averaged as follows: natural events—30% selected the teleofunctional options; natural objects—55% selected the teleofunctional options; animals—45% selected the teleofunctional options; and artifacts—86% selected the teleofunctional options (Kelemen & DiYanni, 2005). For the intelligent design questions, the averages were as follows: natural events—41% selected the intelligent design option; natural objects—42% selected the intelligent design option; animals—66% selected the intelligent design option; and artifacts—87% selected the intelligent design option. "In these closed-ended questions, children exhibited sympathy for someone (an agent) being the cause of that purpose. Features of the natural world, then, are not just accidents that happen to be useful, but are ordered and purposeful" (Barrett, 2012, p. 49).

Of particular interest in the Kelemen and DiYanni (2005) study were the attributions children made about the agent who as responsible for creating the natural world. For natural events, 84% attributed their origins to God, Jesus, or Allah (i.e., theistic attributions); for natural objects, 82% made theistic attributions; for animals, 82% made theistic attributions; and for artifacts 13% made theistic attributions. "For children who offered that some*one* instead of some*thing* was the reason, God was easily a more sensible 'someone' than a human or humans" (Barrett, 2012, p. 64).

Petrovich (1999) also conducted research on children's attributions for the origins of both natural and artificial things. Petrovich showed children photos of both natural and artificial things, asked who made it, and gave children three choices: people, God, or no one knows. "Children in these studies were nearly seven times more likely to answer that God made natural things than people did" (Barrett, 2012, p. 64).

Kelemen and Rosset (2009) expanded the research on promiscuous teleology by determining whether adults might also have such a bias.

Kelemen and Rosset hypothesize that, rather than being limited to a stage of development in childhood, teleological explanations may be the default explanatory tendency throughout all of life. Undergraduate students participated in an experiment where they were randomly assigned into three groups: fast speeded, moderately speeded, and unspeeded. They were given 26 sentences with teleological explanations for scientific phenomena that were inaccurate. The results of the study indicated that the participants in the fast speeded group were most likely to endorse incorrect teleological explanations. The fast speeded group endorsed 47% of the incorrect teleological explanations, the moderately speeded group endorsed 36%, and the unspeeded group endorsed 25%. Summarizing the results, Barrett noted "studies of this sort suggest that we do not simply outgrow the tendency to see purpose in the world but have to learn to tamp it down through formal education, and even then, it comes sneaking out when we are not paying careful attention" (2012, p. 55).

In an effort to determine the extent to which children differentiate between the origins of artifacts and natural items, cognitive psychologist Susan Gelman (1988) "simply asked American children whether a number of different items were made by people: 'Do you think people made lemons?'" (Barrett, 2012, p. 62). Among the four-year-olds participating in the study, 80% said people made artifacts like dolls but not natural items like lemons. A follow-up study that was also designed to test early findings by Piaget, Gelman, and Kremer (1991) asked children to identify who made natural objects like the moon, ocean, and clouds. When Piaget (1929) did his study, he concluded that young children (prior to age 8) tended to view the natural world as being manufactured. Piaget referred to this tendency as *artificialism*. Gelman and Kremer (1991) appear to contradict Piaget's findings. "The results from two studies suggest that children as young as age 4 realize that natural causes exist independently of human influence" (p. 412). Gelman and Kremer's data show that less than 30% of four-year-olds and 10% of seven-year-olds responded with answers consistent with believing natural things we made by humans, or artificialism (Barrett, 2012).

⤶

How Do Children Learn about God?

So how do children learn about God? How do they seem to intuitively know to attribute the creation of natural things to God and the creation of artifacts to humans? Barrett (2012) provides three alternate hypotheses: the *indoctrination hypothesis*, the *anthropomorphism hypothesis*, and the *preparedness hypothesis*.

The *indoctrination hypothesis* is simply that children are taught by their parents and significant others what to believe and how to behave in accordance with those beliefs. Communities of faith have mechanisms in place for formal education through schools, catechism training, etc. Moreover, children hear religious narratives that can both captivate their imagination and communicate religious truth. The story of Jonah and the great fish was not only a whale of a good story but it also taught what happens when you don't do what God tells you to do. However, indoctrination isn't a one-size-fits-all proposition. Some religious ideas are more intuitively grasped by children than others.

E. Margaret Evans (2001) conducted fascinating research with children from both fundamentalist and nonfundamentalist backgrounds, examining their beliefs about origins, namely creationism versus evolution. Evans found that early adolescents tended to accept the dominant beliefs of their community, whether creation or evolution. However, "their younger siblings, especially those in the middle elementary school years (8 to 10 years) were more apt to be exclusively creationist, whatever their community of origin" (Evans, 2001, p. 252). In fact, creationism appears to be more intuitively compatible with how the developing mind works. Evans noted:

> Among nonfundamentalists, a consistent creationism was more likely to be found in the middle elementary school years. Moreover, on most measures of creationism, nonfundamentalist 8- to 10-year-olds were indistinguishable from their fundamentalist counterparts. More revealingly, when asked about the origins of artifacts, the younger nonfundamentalists (5–7 years) were the most likely of all participants to endorse creationist explanations. (p. 256)

For evolutionist communities, this would raise serious questions about the indoctrination hypothesis. Noting that creationist ideas appear to be more easily transmitted, Evans asks, "Why is the human mind (at least, the Western Protestant mind) so susceptible to creationism and so comparatively resistant to naturalistic explanations for the origins of species?" (p. 252). She identifies two possible reasons: *essentialism* and *teleological reasoning*. We have explored the latter in depth. *Essentialism* in this context refers to the belief that species are immutable, endowed with an essence that uniquely identifies members of a species as distinct ontological entities. Essentialism reflects the creation narrative that each species was created by God; evolution is "clearly incommensurate with the idea that a species might change through adaptive processes" (Evans, 2001, p. 254).

The *anthropomorphic hypothesis*, the dominant view of the mainstream psychology of religion, asserts that God is made in man's image (Barrett, 2012). This hypothesis in discussed in the first chapter through Kirkpatrick's (2005) use of attachment theory as an explanation for the development of religion. "Learning god concepts is a simple matter of learning about people and then applying that learning to gods" (Barrett, 2012, p. 79). As the child grows, her god image becomes less like a human and becomes endowed with those qualities associated with the major Abrahamic religions (Judaism, Christianity, and Islam). God becomes "an all-present, formless, unchanging, nontemporal, all-knowing, and all powerful being" (Barrett, 2012, p. 79). Advocates for anthropomorphism, particularly is identifying with a Freudian or Piagetian perspective, necessarily assert that children "are doomed to base their religious concepts on their experience with the concrete world and will therefore not achieve an adult-like capacity for religious belief until they have reached maturity" (Rottman & Kelemen, 2012, p. 208).

Research in infant and child development has accumulated evidence that contradicts the anthropomorphism hypothesis, specifically which infants appear to be sensitive to the characteristics of agency that are attributable to animals, humans, and god. The recognition of agency, thought to be a maturationally natural ability, is a necessary element in believing in supernatural agents, or agents that violate one or more characteristics of their ontological categories. Barrett (2012, p. 34) summarizes these findings as follows:

1. Infants appear to understand that agents can move themselves and other things, an essential prerequisite to successful social interaction.

2. Infants appear to understand that agents can act intentionally to achieve a specific goal.

3. Infants appear to attribute agency to entities that do not resemble humans, "leaving open the possibility that babies could use their same conceptual systems when thinking about gods" (p. 32).

4. Infants appear to attribute agency to entities that are not visible.[2]

These milestones typically occur within the first year and provide the basic elements necessary for thinking about animals, humans, and gods; though they are often invisible and unlike humans in resemblance, gods are both present and active (Barrett, 2012).

The *preparedness hypothesis* (Barrett & Richert, 2003) is one of the variations of what Rottman and Kelemen (2012) refer to as the "strong naturalness theory." Barrett and Richert (2003) assert that the preparedness hypothesis is a valid alternative to anthropomorphism because young children are equipped with the cognitive structures that predispose them to differentiate gods from humans. They contend that these structures have two favorable properties, the first being that "the cognitive device responsible for processing God concepts is a general intention agent device, quite capable of represent human agents as well as any other intentional agent, from God to ghosts to gorillas" (p. 301). Secondly, Barrett and Richert argue that these cognitive structures default to the assumption "that many superhuman properties are the norm" (p. 301). Many children have imaginary friends who possess such qualities as invisibility and omniscience, illustrating the natural tendency to make superhuman attributions to invisible agents (Barrett, 2012).

Rottman and Kelemen (2012) characterize the preparedness hypothesis as flipping anthropomorphism "on its head by asserting that intuitions about agent properties are actually more fit for reasoning about God than for thinking about humans" (p. 210). Empirical research with younger children demonstrates a tendency to over-attribute characteristics like immortality and omniscience to all agents, only later differentiating the human from superhuman as they grow older (Barrett & Richert, 2003; Barrett, 2012; Rottman & Kelemen, 2012).

⤳

Innate Morality in Infancy and Childhood

In addition to having innate faculties that predispose them to a naïve form of religiosity, infants also appear to have an innate capacity for understanding morality. Psychologists Karen Wynn, Paul Bloom, and their colleagues at the Yale Infant Cognition Center have conducted a series of experiments that suggest that infants demonstrate an innate capacity for moral cognition. Based on lab findings, Wynn (2008) proposes three innate capacities that equip infants to function morally and, by extension, socially, since morality is as an aspect of social interaction. First, infants are capable of employing separate cognitive systems when engaging the physical and social worlds. For the former, they are able to apply an understanding of naive physics, while with the social world, they "view the actions of intentional agents as ontologically different from the actions of inanimate objects . . . [making] 'essentialist' inferences about the source of behavior of intentional agents, viewing their actions as arising from intrinsic, essential features, not superficial or extrinsic attributes" (Wynn, 2008, p. 330). Second, Wynn's experimental findings suggest that infants interpret the behavior of social beings, or agents, as the result of those agents' goals or desires: "infants' earliest understanding of social entities and their interactions involves reference to the mental contents and states of the actors" (Wynn, 2008, p. 330). Third, Wynn contends that infants observing social interactions also judge those interactions as being either good or bad.

How, you might wonder, can the researchers at the Yale Infant Cognition Center make such assertions about infants? Except for certain precocious infants in television and the movies, infants can't tell us what they are thinking about an agent's behavior. One experimental method employed is termed *looking-time* (Bloom, 2013). Babies are capable of controlling their gaze, and novel or surprising stimuli are likely to engage their gaze longer than stimuli that are routine or uninteresting. Another method is reaching, or a *choice paradigm*, where infants indicate a preference for a specific stimulus by reaching for it from among offered stimuli (Hamlin, Wynn, & Bloom, 2007). One experiment involved 6- and 10-month-old babies watching a small wooden "character" trying to climb a hill. After the "climber" makes two attempts, children were shown alternating scenarios, where in one scenario the climber is aided by a helper, while in the second scenario the climber is obstructed by a hinderer. Infants were then presented with both the helper and hinderer and asked to reach for one. Of the 16 10-month-olds participating, 14 choose the helper; similarly, of the 12 6-month-olds participating, all choose the helper. The statistical probability of these choices being due to random error was very, very low.[3] This study was repeated with three-month-olds, where the looking method was substituted for the reaching method. As with the experiment with the six- and ten-month-olds, the three-month-olds preferred looking at the helper rather than the hinderer (Bloom, 2013; Hamlin, Wynn, & Bloom, 2007).

Another study (Hamlin & Wynn, 2011) originating from the Yale Infant Cognition Center attempted to replicate the results with different scenarios (cited in Bloom, 2013). In one scenario, a character tries to open the lid of a box. A helper would open the lid for the character, while a hinderer would slam the lid shut. In a second scenario, a character plays with a ball, which rolls away. A helper rolls the ball back, while a hinderer ran away with it. "In both situations, five-month-olds preferred the good guy—the one who helped to open the box, the one who rolled the ball back—to the bad guy" (Bloom, 2013, p. 30).

Bloom suggests that moral reasoning is both innate and complex, involving not only moral judgments, but also "a desire to help others in need, compassion for those in pain, anger toward the cruel, and guilt and pride about our own shameful and kind actions" (Bloom, 2013, p. 31). How might these innate faculties, arguably the product of modules associated with moral and social interaction, relate to religion? Boyer contends the reason is that "gods and spirits and ancestors are generally considered *interested parties* in moral choices and mortal judgments, rather than providers of codes and rules" (Boyer, 2001, p. 189). Inasmuch as infants make intuitive judgments about moral behavior, so also would gods, who are assumed to have similar moral concerns. Moreover, inasmuch as these supernatural agents are both interested parties and all-knowing, they would know what would need to be known about situations or circumstances and, as interested parties in the adjudication of morality, make the appropriate judgments, which often include consequences. This appears most appropriately attributed to gods that are omniscient, omnipresent, and omnipotent, as is the God of Judaism, Christianity, and Islam (Barrett, 2012). "The combination of being superknowing and superperceiving and supremely powerful may rest comfortably with a being morally good as well—at least better than a fairly stupid and uninformed, weak god" (Barrett, 2012, p. 123).[4]

Barrett (2004) offers a synthesis for the faculties for innate moral judgments, the innate faculties for belief in supernatural agents, and unexpected fortune or misfortune. Recently, *USA Today* contained a report detailing how lightning from an isolated thunderstorm on an otherwise hot and sunny day at Venice Beach in California killed one person, a 20-year-old man, and injured several others (Welch, 2014). Fatal lightning strikes are relatively uncommon occurrences and tend to attract the public's attention. Barrett contends that such occurrences are traces that activate the HADD, intuitively leading us to look for agents responsible. "Gods, by virtue of their strange physical properties and their mysterious superpowers, make fine candidates for causes of many of these unusual events" (Barrett, 2004, p. 52). In addition to activating the HADD, attributions of agency also activates what Pyysiäinen (2009) calls the *hyperactive understanding of intentionality* and what Barrett (2004) calls the *social exchange regulator*. When encountering a lightning strike, these tools intuitively provoke us to look for agency, intentionality, and evidence of reciprocity. Upon reflection, we can offer an alternative explanation based primarily on a physical explanation, namely that thunderstorms contain lightning and lightning strikes unpredictably and sometimes unavoidably. The unfortunate young man just happened to be at the wrong place at the wrong time. The important point is to recognize that our innate, intuitive faculties are activated rapidly and automatically; it is only upon reflection that we are able to make a judgment as to the accuracy or inaccuracy of our initial impressions. Barrett (2004) summarizes the exercise of these mental tools in the face of surprising misfortune:

> Our mental tools . . . 1) look for a cause for surprising misfortune, 2) incline toward agentive/social explanations related to reward/punishment exchanges, but 3) require that a candidate agent could reasonably know about the evil that was done, even in secret, and has the power to punish. (p. 54)

The story of Ananias and Sapphira in the New Testament Acts of the Apostles offers an instructive demonstration of the above. In Acts 4:32–36, the author tells of how the believers shared everything, with no one claiming personal property. The believers sold their homes and property and laid the money at the feet of the apostles. Acts 5, however, offers a cautionary tale. Ananias and Sapphira were members of this early community. They sold property but instead of giving all the money to the apostles, they conspired to keep some and give the rest. The apostle Peter, acting as God's agent, knew what they had done in secret. He confronted Ananias, saying "You have not lied to man but to God" (Acts 5:4c, ESV). Upon hearing Peter's words, Ananias fell down dead. Three hours later, his wife Sapphira, unaware of what had happened, is also confronted by Peter. She maintained the lie and also dropped dead. The moral nexus of the story is that they both attempted to deceive God and the others by not reciprocating and giving the full proceeds of their sale, as the others had done. The moral judgment was swift and irrevocable.

SUMMARY

- Piaget's cognitive development model has provided a foundation for other developmental models of religion. Piaget theorized that children move through four stages: the sensorimotor stage, the preoperational stage, the operational stage, and formal operations. With each stage, children progress through a series of developmental milestones that enable their thinking to become more sophisticated and abstract.

- Based on the analysis of about 800 children's drawings, Ernest Harms and his colleagues classified three stages of religious experience: the fairy-tale stage, the realistic stage, and the individualistic stage. These stages roughly share similar characteristics of the last three stages of Piaget's cognitive development model.

- David Elkind theorizes that children's religious beliefs emerge through cognitive development in the form of cognitive need capacities. Each of Piaget's stages creates a tension between the child and her environment that are expressed as needs, which are then resolved through aspects of institutional religion. These cognitive need capacities are conservation, representation, relation, and comprehension, which are resolved through the God concept, Scripture, worship, and theology, respectively.

- James Fowler's faith development model attempts to integrate multiple developmental models into an integrated whole. After identifying a pre-stage (undifferentiated faith), Fowler proposes the following stages that correspond to the human lifespan: intuitive-projective, mythic-literal, individuative-reflective, conjunctive, and universalizing. Fowler contends that many adults remain in the mythic-literal stage and that universalizing faith is very rare.

- Heinz Streib offers an alternative to Fowler's stage development in reconceptualizing the stages as styles. Believing the stage development model relies too heavily on Enlightenment rationalism, Streib believes that styles allow for a more flexible and integrative approach. Streib does not offer an analog for the undifferentiated faith of infants and begins his model with the subjective religious style, which corresponds with Fowler's intuitive-projective stage of faith. Subsequent styles correspond with each of Fowler's stages: instrumental-reciprocal, mutual religious, and dialogical religious, which encompasses both the conjunctive and universalizing stages of Fowler's model.

- The cognitive faculties necessary for religious cognition emerge naturally as a result of normal maturation, a process McCauley calls *maturational naturalness*. Barrett (2012) contends that there are several maturationally natural cognitive processes that constitute the foundation of religious thinking, including *teleological functioning*, *intelligent design attribution*, or the belief that *someone* rather than *something* or *nothing* is responsible for creating natural things like birds or lemons, and the superhuman agency of God, or the belief that God functions superhumanly regarding perception and omniscience, moral judgment, and immortality.

- Barrett (2012) offers three alternate hypotheses for how children learn about God: the *indoctrination hypothesis*, the *anthropomorphism hypothesis*, and the *preparedness hypothesis*.
- Wynn, Bloom and other researchers at the Yale Infant Cognition Center have conducted a series of experiments that suggest that infants demonstrate an innate capacity for moral cognition. Infants as young as three-months-old show preferences for good agents over bad agents.

NOTES

[1] There are many developmental models of religion, but a review of those is beyond the scope of this book. Our emphasis will be on those developmental models that rely primarily or exclusively on cognition.

[2] For a more in-depth exploration of this research, refer to Barrett (2012) and Rottman and Kelemen (2012).

[3] It is .2% for the 10-month-old group and .02% for the 6-month-old group (Hamlin, Wynn, & Bloom, 2007).

[4] Barrett uses the term "gods" to describe any supernatural agent. Cognitive anthropologist Harvey Whitehouse (1996) provides an example of a limited god in the *sega*, who are the forest spirits of the Baining people of Papua New Guinea. Their knowledge is limited to what they observe in the forest and otherwise have no access to information needed to make moral judgments.

6

The Social-Cognitive Processes of Religious Transmission

QUESTIONS TO BE ADDRESSED

1. How do some religious ideas become accepted worldwide while others do not?
2. How do religions correspond to the two fundamental aspects of human existence: information and cooperation?
3. In what ways are religious ideas like epidemics?
4. What makes a religious idea contagious?
5. In what ways do memes, cognitive analogs for genes, effectively transmit ideas?
6. In what ways can religious ideas be either *cognitively optimal* or *cognitively costly*?
7. How do the doctrinal and imagistic modes of religiosity differ?

Memorable Narratives

Imagine hearing the following story: "A girl and a boy, sister and brother, were walking home from school on an ordinary day in an ordinary town. As they were walking towards home, they came upon a dog belonging to one of their friends" (Barrett & Nyhof, 2001, p. 97). It is doubtful that you would find this memorable or repeat it to others. There is nothing interesting or novel—no interesting inferences, no implicit reference to the deep questions of human existence, nothing mysterious or supernatural. Imagine telling a friend or loved one this story. They would look at you, waiting for the rest of the story. What might have made this story more memorable? What if the next line of the story was, "The dog crouched on the front lawn as it composed a symphony" (Barrett & Nyhof, 2001, p. 97)? Now, that *is* interesting: a dog composing a symphony—perhaps something like *Canine Cantata*.

Consider a second example. A man shepherding his flock of sheep in the wilderness encounters a burning bush. The bush is quickly consumed by the fire; end of story. Again, this is nothing out of the ordinary. However, Moses's encounter with the burning bush in Exodus 3 not only begins the narrative of the Jews' deliverance from slavery in Egypt, but also introduces us to the God of the Hebrews, Yahweh, a name revered so greatly that devout Jews only use the Hebrew term *hashem*, or THE NAME.

While there are obvious differences between the two narratives, both are memorable for their violations of their respective ontological categories. Intuitively we expect dogs to scratch or dig and bushes to burn up when on fire. These anomalies are novel and activate those cognitive modules designed to make sense out of them. Because of their memorability, these events are also more likely to be transmitted to others. What makes some ideas more likely to be successfully transmitted while others are not? In the fourth season of the animated television comedy *Family Guy*, Peter (the family guy) decides to form the Church of the Fonz, a religion based on his favorite television hero Arthur "the Fonz" Fonzarelli, the über-cool character in the television series *Happy Days*. Unfortunately, the Church of the Fonz disbanded when members were recruited away to join other, more compelling churches. How do some religions become world religions while others, like the Church of the Fonz, fail?

In his classic book on the world religions, Huston Smith (1958/1991) addresses a significant historical question on what made Judaism a world religion. According to Smith, the Hebrews were minor players in the geopolitical world of antiquity, yet became the vehicle for a world religion that would forge that Judeo-Christian ethos of the West for at least two millennia. Smith asserts that "what lifted the Jews from obscurity to permanent religious greatness was their passion for meaning" (p. 272), specifically finding their meaning in their understanding of God. The Jewish understanding of God was a robust account of the "other." Smith elaborates that "no one seriously claims to be self-created, and as they are not, other people (being likewise human) did not bring themselves into being either. From this it follows that humankind has issued from something other than itself" (p. 272). For the Jews, the Other was the culmination of monotheism, a superordinate deity that transcended all of creation, unlike the deities of their neighbors that were restricted to specific domains like the sea or wind. Moreover, the God of the Hebrews was unlike the other deities in character. "It is here that we come to the supreme achievement of Jewish thought—not in its monotheism as such, but in the character it ascribed to the God it intuited as One" (Smith, 1958/1991, p. 275). How? The God of the Hebrews cared deeply for His people, heard their cries of distress in bondage in Egypt, and delivered them. Smith makes this succinct distinction: "Whereas the gods of Olympus tirelessly pursued beautiful women, the God of Sinai watched over orphans and widows" (p. 275).

It is not insignificant that Judaism, according to Smith, flourished because of its emphasis on meaning. Judaism provided not only an explanatory framework for God, but also for creation, human existence, morality, justice, and suffering. As you have observed with the previously-discussed child development research, children are meaning-makers, sometimes promiscuously, as Kelemen (1999) notes. Human cognitive architecture appears well-suited to understanding mental representations consistent with a monotheistic religion, certainly more so than a religion based on a television comedy set in the 1950s. The spread of Judaism owes itself to the ease with which these mental representations are similarly generated throughout the culture.

The fundamentals of Judaism illustrate two aspects of human existence without which it would be difficult, if not impossible, for humans to survive: information and cooperation (Boyer, 2001). Our brains are designed to constantly process feedback from our environments; human beings are in dynamic interaction with our environments such that each modifies the other. We are always both adapting to our environments and adapting our environments to better suit us. Inasmuch as organisms have specific environmental niches which maximizes their ability to thrive, humans appear to require what anthropologists call a *cognitive niche* (Boyer, 2001). "Just as frogs need ponds and whales need seawater, humans are constantly immersed in a milieu that is indispensable to their operation and survival, and that milieu is information-about-the-environment" (p. 121). Judaism offered abundant amounts of meaningful information that helped explain otherwise inscrutable phenomena. The existence of an omniscient and omnipotent God permits inferences about creation, morality, and suffering. These inferences became formally incorporated into a system that included rituals, ceremonies, feasts, and an oral tradition that facilitated transmission to subsequent generations (Sterelny, 2006).

Cooperation is also an essential aspect of survival within humanity's cognitive niche. "Humans need cooperation because they depend on rich information, well beyond what individual experience can provide. Other people provide most of this information" (Boyer, 2001, p. 121). Most importantly, Boyer (2001) notes, humans need information about what is in other people's minds—what they know, what they intend to do with that knowledge, what their motivations and desires are, etc. Hence, the cognitive niche is primarily social and activates the cognitive tools that coordinate social activity, like the mental tools identified by Barrett (2004): the *social exchange regulator*, a mental tool designed to determine social obligations, and the *social status monitor*, a mental tool that identifies high-status members of a community with whom an alliance may be formed and from whom information may be reliably gained.

The Ten Commandments, or the so-called Decalogue, as given directly by Moses are traditionally divided into three sections. Commandments 1–4 provide the laws that govern the Jews' relationship with God, commandments 6–10 provide the laws that govern relationships with one another. Prohibitions against murder, adultery, theft, bearing false witness, and covetousness obviously promote cooperation among the members of a community. The fifth commandment, "Honor your father and your mother, that your days may be long in the land that the LORD your God is giving you" (Exodus 20:12, ESV), serves as a bridge between the two sections (Johnson, 1987) and is an excellent illustration of Barrett's social exchange regulator. Honor is given to parents in exchange for living long in the land. Johnson notes that the Decalogue was singular in the covenants made in the ancient Near East. "But the Mosaic covenant is unique in being, not a treaty between states, but a God-people alliance. In it, in effect, the ancient Israelite society merged its interests with God's and accepted Him, in return for protection and prosperity" (Johnson, 1987, p. 35).

∽

Mental Epidemics

Several scholars use an *epidemiological framework* to conceptualize culture. The term *epidemiological* may be surprising at first, since it is often associated with the spread of biological contagion. The Centers for Disease Control and Prevention in the United States recently advised against nonessential travel to Sierra Leone, Liberia, and Guinea "because of an unprecedented outbreak of Ebola" (CDC, 2014). Ebola is a virulent virus that is often fatal to those it infects. The challenge epidemiologists face is how to impede the spread of such a virus, particularly when cultural practices related to preparation for burial or inadequate medical training contribute to spreading the contagion.

In certain respects, mental representations are to the mind what viruses are to the body. Mental representations become cultural when they "are widely and durably distributed in a social group" (Sperber, 1996, p. 49). Tooby and Cosmides (1992) use the term *epidemiological culture* to describe the cognitive and social processes involved in the distribution of successful ideas. Inasmuch as the human immune system has the biological architecture prone to infection from biological contagion, human cognitive architecture is prone to the absorption of ideas, some of which are more easily absorbed than others.

Similarly, Sperber (1996) explains culture as an "epidemiology of representation" (1996, p. 50), resulting from how individuals form and modify mental representations, and how these mental representations are transmitted from one mind to another. Tooby and Cosmides (1992) contend that transmission occurs through the use of *inference*. "Observer's inferential mechanisms construct representations similar to those present in others; domain-specific mechanism influence which representations spread through a population easily and which do not" (p. 121). One well-known example of such inferential mechanisms is Noam Chomsky's hypothesis that the facility for human language is based on an innate universal grammar that facilitates the rapid development of linguistic capability (Boyd & Richerson, 2006). In essence, epidemical cognitive contagia are those that facilitate rapid inferential processes on the part of the recipient such that the mental representations they construct are approximate to the mental representations of the sender. Specifically, cognitive architecture is *modular,* or *domain-specific* (see chapter 4). Modularity suggests "that a specific brain mechanism is dedicated to processing a specific kind of information (Jeeves & Brown, 2009, p. 60), like facial recognition. Inasmuch as these specific brain mechanisms or modules operate rapidly and efficiently, they facilitate the spread of mental representations.

Boyer (2001) contends that "religion is a particular kind of mental epidemic whereby people develop (on the basis of variable information) rather similar forms of religious concepts and norms" (p. 47). Boyer does not intend the term "mental epidemic" in a pejorative sense. An epidemic emerges when multiple people demonstrate a cluster of symptoms in response to a particular pathogenic agent. Bodies respond in similar ways because they have innate infection-response systems. Similarly, religious beliefs emerge in response to particular religiogenic agents (specific types of mental representations) because our minds have innate faculties to do so. Specifically, Boyer argues that we all share templates for religious concepts. In other words, all human beings have faculties "that build religious concepts by producing inferences on the basis of some information provided by other people and by experience" (p. 47).

Tremlin (2006) offers three reasons why the epidemiological model of culture is an optimal metaphor. First, those ideas and values that constitute culture are like biological contagion because both are shared across the group. Also, like biological contagion, ideas and values reside within individuals and are spread through the contagious medium of communication. Second, the so-called "pathogens" of culture are ideas that exist within the minds of individuals and are spread to the minds of other individuals, much like biological pathogens are spread by one person infecting another person. "Third, epidemiological models in general recognize that macro-scale effects are the result of micro-scale causes. One infectious person begins an epidemic: one clever notion starts a fad" (Tremlin, 2006, p. 149).

Sperber (1996) makes some important distinctions about mental representations. First, it is not enough to say that something represents something; instead, "something represents something *for someone*" [italics added] (p. 78). Moreover, Sperber differentiates between *internal representations* that include idiosyncratic memories and impressions, and *public representations*, like familiar sayings or symbols "which are material phenomena in the environment of people and which represent something for people who perceive and interpret them" (Sperber, 1996, p. 78). While the former may exist wholly within an individual's mind and remain there, the latter is widely shared by members. More specifically, Sperber clarifies that to share a public representation is "that these individuals have mental representations similar enough to be considered versions of one another" (p. 82).

Sperber (1996) also makes a distinction between two kinds of beliefs: *intuitive* and *reflective*. This distinction is also made by Barrett, who uses the terms *nonreflective* and *reflective*. Intuitive/nonreflective beliefs are those that occur rapidly and automatically without conscious reflection. A typical five-month-old has a working knowledge of intuitive physics when she knows that balls or shoes must be contacted in order to start moving (Barrett, 2012). Sperber (1996) contends that intuitive beliefs are acquired through perception and/or communication.

> Take the widespread intuitive belief that coal is black: were you told it, or did you infer it from your own perception? Hard to know. But even if you inferred it from perception, in doing so you used the concept of black and coal, and how did you acquire those? (p. 94)

Knowledge of the color black, Sperber contends, is innate, so by learning the word for the color you acquire a means to label it. Knowledge of coal itself is not innate, but the ontological category to which a lump of coal belongs carries with it expectations for physical objects: solidity, color, shape, cohesiveness, etc. Therefore, when you were first introduced to this particular type of sedimentary rock and learned the word "coal" you automatically associated the color black with it. You may have even told someone else with breathless amazement, "did you know coal was black?" Maybe not.

How do intuitive beliefs differ in distribution from reflective beliefs? Sperber (1996) contends that "whereas widespread intuitive beliefs owe their distribution both to common perceptual experiences and to communication, widespread reflective beliefs owe theirs almost exclusively to communication" (pp. 94–95). What constitutes successful communication of reflective beliefs? For Sperber (1996), it depends on the reflective belief. For myths, factors include memorability, attractiveness, and the authority of the communicator. For political beliefs, factors include individual relevance and institutional acceptance. For complex abstractions like scientific theories or mathematical formulas, factors involve the ability to understand the particulars.

The three types of reflective beliefs to which Sperber refers may coalesce around religion. If we consider myths broadly as either historic or symbolic representations of important religious concepts, we can see where the factors of memorability, attractiveness, and authority apply. Consider Jesus's parable of the Good Samaritan (Luke 10:25–37). First, as a parable, it was not intended to be an historic narrative of an actual event. Second, it is a memorable (and therefore attractive) story. A lawyer asks Jesus what he needs to do to inherit eternal life. Jesus responds by asking him to repeat what was written in the Law, which includes the injunction to love his neighbor as himself. After reciting the Law, the lawyer, seeking a loophole, asks Jesus, "And who is my neighbor?" Jesus answers with a parable about the good Samaritan. What is attractive and memorable about the story is that an Israelite was beaten and left for dead. Both a priest and a Levite ignored the injured man, but a Samaritan (despised by the Israelites) took it upon himself to bind his wounds and pay for his care at an inn until he returned. The beaten man's neighbors were not his fellow countryman but the Samaritan, who showed him mercy. Insofar as authority is concerned, Jesus had already established this among the people ("And when Jesus finished these sayings, the crowds were astonished at his teaching, for he was teaching them as one who had authority, and not as their scribes," Matthew 7:28–29, ESV).

Consider the philosophical and existential issues to which Huston Smith (1958/1991) refers in theorizing how Judaism became a world religion. Concepts like a superordinate God who cares for his people, the mysteries of creation and human existence addressed in the Creation narrative, and the ability to put morality, justice, and suffering into a broader theological narrative were all very relevant to ancient people struggling to make sense of an otherwise chaotic world. Moreover, all of these concepts were embedded in a theological framework that required its believers to understand such complexities as an omniscient, omnipotent, and omnipresent deity who is both judge and savior.

Boyer offers an excellent illustration of the epidemiological nature of beliefs in his work with the Fang people of Cameroon and Gabon (Boyd & Richerson, 2006). Boyer reports that many of his Fang acquaintances told of seeing animals in the forest suddenly disappear without a trace. Their interpretation of this event was that a ghost had taken the animal. For the Fang, ghosts are menacing spirits that haunt the forests and otherwise inexplicable events are attributed to ghosts. The Fang's "ghost-concept is mostly informed by constant warnings of the wandering spirits' menacing presence" (Boyer, 2001, p. 148). In fact, Boyer contends, this communication is enough to cement a belief in the existence and danger of ghosts, regardless of whether individual members of the Fang people actually encounter one. Boyer's experiences with the Fang illustrate the epidemiological nature of learning about ghosts. Once the mental representation of ghosts replete with all their counterintuitiveness is communicated, the cognitive architecture innate in all Fang, and all people for that matter, readily recreates the mental representation. "Once young Fang children learn that ghosts are sentient beings, they don't need to learn that ghosts can see or that they have beliefs and desires— these components are provided by cognitive machinery that reliably develops in every environment" (Boyd & Richerson, 2006, p. 28).

༄

Transmission of Counterintuitive Concepts

What makes an idea contagious? Simply, it is easy to remember and has a conceptual structure that requires a modest amount of cognitive effort to understand it; it fits within the cognitive templates we innately possess for understanding our environment. For example, a talking fish is more contagious than just a fish, or a fish that plays the accordion, eats airplanes, vanishes every Thursday, and turns into a rock whenever the moon is full (Barrett, 2004). This example demonstrates differentiates among three types of concepts: intuitive (fish), minimally counterintuitive (talking fish), and maximally counterintuitive (accordion-playing, airplane-eating, Thursday-vanishing, rock-morphing fish). As discussed previously, a minimally counterintuitive concept is one where most of its attributes are consistent with the ontological category to which it belongs while possessing one or two violations. A talking fish is consistent with most attributes associated with the ANIMATE ontological category except for intelligible speech, which is a transfer of attributes from the PERSON category. These differentiations are significant because religious concepts typically contain minimally counterintuitive attributes (Atran, 2002; Barrett, 2004; Boyer, 2001). In other words, they violate the expectations associated with their respective ontological category; they are expectation-incongruent concepts.

A series of experiments were designed to test Boyer's (1994) hypothesis that "concepts that have a property that violates intuitive assumptions for that thing's category membership will be better remembered and *transmitted* than other concepts" (Barrett & Nyhof, 2001, p. 73). The first study sought to reexamine the findings of a seminal study in memory conducted by Frederic C. Bartlett using an American indian folktale "The War of the Ghosts" (1932). Bartlett's experiment is described as follows:

> Bartlett had subjects read the story and then retell the tale in writing. These retellings were then read and retold by other subjects. Over several generations of retellings, Bartlett reported that culturally unfamiliar concepts became distorted to better fit cultural schema, while other nonschematic concepts were forgotten. Most strikingly, Bartlett observed that . . . the concept of ghost had been eliminated over the course of ten retellings. (Barrett & Nyhof, 2001, p. 73)

In the Barrett and Nyhof study (2001), half of the 48 participants read and retold one set of three Native American folktales, the other half read a separate set. The folktales all contained both intuitive and counterintuitive elements. Barrett and Nyhof hypothesized that the counterintuitive elements would be better remembered and more accurately told than the intuitive elements. One example from the folktales used in the experiment involved a grandmother's bones returning home singing and two children transforming themselves into a burning stick and blue stone. Their hypothesis was supported; the counterintuitive concepts were recalled 60.4% of the time, while the intuitive concepts were recalled 43.3% of the time. The difference between the two percentages was statistically significant, indicating the differences have a very low probability of being due to random sampling error.[1]

The second experiment involved a story with a controlled number of counterintuitive and intuitive elements. "The story described an intergalactic ambassador's visit to a museum on another world. . . . This museum had 18 exhibits: six that illustrated various types of physical objects, six that illustrated various types of living things, and six that illustrated various types of intentional agents" (Barrett & Nyhof, 2001, p. 78). The study sought to determine how well the exhibits were remembered and transmitted from telling to retelling. Each of the item categories (objects, living, things, intentional agents) possessed one of the following properties: counterintuitive, bizarre, and ordinary. Bizarre items are defined as items that "possessed a highly unusual feature that violates no category-level assumptions but may violate basic-level regularities" (p. 78). A dog weighing five tons is highly irregular, but not counterintuitive because living things can weigh five tons (e.g., a southern elephant seal). The account of the ambassador's visit was read and retold through multiple generations. The results suggested that counterintuitive items were better remembered and transmitted than the bizarre or common items. There were limitations that Barret and Nyhof noted in the study: participants read the narrative "while traditionally, stories and cultural concepts are transmitted orally" (p. 83). In addition, "recall was only examined immediately following transmission, whereas in natural settings transmission of a concept may occur long after exposure to the concept" (p. 83). Finally, the methodology was only an approximate approach to cultural transmission; "real world transmission involves actual face to face interactions, hearing different versions from multiple speakers, and the effects of telling stories multiple times" (p. 84). In their third and fourth experiments, Barrett and Nyhof sought to replicate a small cultural group. A subset of the group was told a story and then asked to initiate a series of retellings to other members of the group.

The third experiment involved a narrative involving a sister and brother walking home from school and encountering six minimally counterintuitive items and six intuitive items. The minimally counterintuitive items included a dog composing a symphony, a jumping rose, and a talking carrot. The intuitive items including a slimy earthworm, an aromatic shrub, and a red picket fence. The results continued to support their initial hypothesis. Counterintuitive items were remembered significantly better than intuitive items after immediate exposure. Results were similar after a three-month delay; while the overall percentage of items recalled was lower than after immediate recall, the counterintuitive items were remembered significantly better than the intuitive items. The fourth experiment was similar, though the intuitive items were replaced with bizarre items. For example, a bright pink newspaper replaced a crumpled newspaper. As with the third experiment, the counterintuitive items were remembered significantly better than the bizarre items both upon immediate recall and after a three-month delay. An interesting phenomenon occurred during the recall of bizarre items. Participants tended to recall bizarre items as counterintuitive items. For example, "of the ten participants who remembered the newspaper, six recalled it as walking or running, not blowing in the wind" (Barrett & Nyhof, 2001, p. 89). Barrett and Nyhof (2001) concluded that the four experiments supported "Boyer's theory that counterintuitive concepts have transmission advantages that account for the commonness and ease of communicating many non-natural cultural concepts" (p. 91).

Memes

When most of this current generation thinks of memes, they are likely to think of Internet images of kittens or babies. To some extent, this is correct. Memes are defined as "units of culture, notions, values, stories, etc., that get people to speak or act in certain ways that make other people store a replicated version of these mental units" (Boyer, 2001, p. 35). Memes function like genes; genes are biological duplication programs that transmit themselves from generation to generation. Similarly, memes are cultural duplication programs that also facilitate transmission.

The notion of *memes* was popularized in Richard Dawkins's 1976 book *The Selfish Gene*. Dawkins describes genes as replication programs designed to perpetuate their likenesses, leaping "from body to body down the generations, manipulating body after body in its own way and for its own ends, abandoning a succession of mortal bodies before they [the bodies] sink in senility and death" (Dawkins, 1976, p. 36). The gene's success is determined by how well it manipulates those bodies in which it dwells before being passed on, or leaping, to subsequent generations (Dawkins, 1978). Like genes, memes are replicators of cultural ideas, otherwise known as *units of imitation* (Greene, 1978). Examples are legion, including words, phrases, proverbs, dances, tunes, rituals, jokes, table manners, theories, equations, etc. (Atran, 2002; Boyer, 2001). Although nonbiological, they undergo Darwinian selection like genes. "Cultures and religions are supposedly coalitions of memes seeking to maximize their own fitness, regardless of fitness costs for their human hosts" (Atran, 2002, p. 236). Hence, a meme "spreads not because it is advantageous to either the group or to the individual, but rather because it is advantageous to itself" (Greene, 1978, p. 709). One example Dawkins (1976) offers of a self-perpetuating meme is hell fire, speculating that the reason for its persistence in the meme pool is "because of its own deep psychological impact" (p. 212). As a so-called "copy-me" program (Dawkins, 1976), a meme is communicated from one person to the next, which in turn provokes a behavioral response. You tell the one about the chicken crossing the road to your friend, who hears it, stores it in memory, and repeats the joke to someone else; in other words, there is a cycle of acquisition of the meme, storage and retrieval in memory, and communication (Boyer, 2001). This cycle perpetuates itself throughout a population.

If memes are analogous to genes in terms of survival through natural selection, successful replication and transmission involves both the *fertility* of the meme and the *fidelity* of its reproductions (Atran, 2002). Fertile memes are those memes that are successfully and abundantly transmitted, being more suited for acquisition by the modular architecture of the human mind (Atran, 2002).

> This would be why so many people in different cultures think that invisible spirits lurk around and so few imagine that their internal organs change location during the night, why the notion of moralistic ancestors watching your behavior is more frequent than that of immoral ghosts who want you to steal from your neighbors. (Boyer, 2001, p. 37)

Fidelity is where the analogy runs into problems. While genes usually render faithful reproductions of themselves, memes do not. "On the contrary, the process of transmission seems guaranteed to create an extraordinary profusion of baroque variations" (Boyer, 2001, p. 38). You may remember playing the telephone game with a large group of people where one person whispers a phrase to someone, who whispers what they thought they heard to the next person, and so forth. The concluding phrase is often quite different from the starting one. "Dance like no one is watching" could easily become "Dense like Noah the watch king." *Mondegreens* are a similar phenomenon. The word derives from a 1954 article written by Sylvia Wright in *Harper's Magazine* where she recounts how she misheard a portion of a stanza from the Scottish ballad "The Bonnie Earl o' Moray." The lyrics actually read "They have slain the Earl o' Moray/ And layd him on the green." As a child, Wright instead misheard the last line as "And the Lady Mondegreen." She writes of developing a detailed image of the two slain nobles, pierced with arrows and resplendent in fine clothes befitting of their noble status (Conner, 2009). Gavin Edwards writes that as a child he heard that last line of "Row, Row, Row Your Boat" as "Life's a butter dream" (Edwards, 2013). Edwards goes on to write that "mondegreens can be found in every area of the spoken word, from the record-buyer who asks for a copy of the Queen single 'Bohemian Rap City' to the schoolchild who is convinced that the Pledge of Allegiance begins 'I led the pigeons to the flag'" (2013, para. 5).

Boyer writes of how Dawkins's own concepts from *The Selfish Gene* (1976) demonstrate both the faithful replication of memes and their distortion. Not long after the book was published, "virtually everybody in the social sciences and in evolutionary biology or psychology knew about it and for the most part had an essentially correct notion of the original meaning" (Boyer, 2001, p. 38). Conversely, the idea of the selfish gene, the eponymous subject of Dawkins's book, was distorted in transmission. Dawkins use of the term "selfish gene" was to describe that the sole purpose of the gene is to ensure its survival and replicate itself. Instead, the "selfish gene" meme became the gene that makes us selfish (Boyer, 2001). Boyer explains that the distortion is understandable "because people had a prior notion that the phrase 'selfish gene' seemed to match. The original explanation (the original meme) was completely ignored, the better to fit that prior conception" (Boyer, 2001, p. 39).

Apart from the examples cited above, cultural transmission of memes not only involves changes from person to person, but also changes *within* the mind of the person (Boyer, 2001). Once in the mind, a meme is elaborated on, connected with other memes, modified to fit specific expectations, etc. Sperber (1996) contends that mental representations like memes don't simply replicate themselves in transmission, they transform. The information processing view of the mind-as-computer does a disservice to understanding memetic transmission. Memes are not downloaded from one mind to another, nor are they like data transmitted from one computer to the next.

> The main difference between minds that communicate and computers that route e-mail is that minds *never* swallow raw information to serve it to others in the same raw state. Minds invariably do a lot of work, *especially so* when transmission is faithful. . . . In human communication, *good transmission requires as much work as does distortion.* (Boyer, 2001, pp. 39–40)

The error in the metaphor involves the process of replication (Atran, 2002; Boyer, 2001; Tremlin, 2006). Atran (2002) notes that the transmission of ideas rarely occurs without significant modification. Instead of being copying machines, brains interpret external ideas according to an existing explanatory framework, some of which is innate and some based on experience (Tremlin, 2006). "The real mystery is how any group of people manages an effective degree of common understanding given that transformation of ideas during transmission is the rule rather than the exception" (Atran, 2002, p. 241).

Atran (2002) offers a religious example of low-fidelity transmission in the Golden Rule: Do unto others as you would have them do unto you. Since memes are ideas that stimulate behavioral responses, the Golden Rule

> can mean very different things to different people even within the same local congregation and can mean different things to the same person at different times. Sometimes [it] may suggest noninterference in one another's affairs; at other times, it may be involved as a call for mutual assistance. (p. 251)

Nonetheless, the Golden Rule has remained a potent and understandable concept since its inception. Its essence is based on the human qualities of empathy and reciprocity. Despite the various ways in which it can be expressed, the meme itself appears quite robust. "The crucial element of a meme-based theory is that the fitness of the memes themselves plays a crucial explanatory role" (Sterelny, 2006, p. 155).

Boyer (2001) suggests that the fitness of a meme is based on *relevance*, which by definition refers to memes that allow multiple inferences (e.g., the crops failed because we angered our ancestors, the bunyip turned the villagers into crows because they stole her cub) or which fit the expectations of whatever cognitive template is activated by the meme without excessive amount of cognitive effort. Acquiring these memes is nearly inevitable. "We do not have the cultural concepts we have because they make sense or are useful but because the way our brains are put together makes it very difficult *not* to build them [italics added]" (Boyer, 2001, p. 164). In fact, Tremlin (2006) argues that humans across culture share a universal psychology that functions based on biologically-based rules that are species-specific. "'Religion' is a pancultural phenomenon precisely because all people everywhere are naturally predisposed to acquire it" (p. 145).

As it relates to religion, memes that require less cognitive effort are those associated with the social aspect of religiosity. As mentioned previously, humans require social information in order to exist cooperatively. Information like knowing to whom loyalty or allegiance is owed, knowing what public rituals to perform, or knowing which other members of the community are or are not as knowledgeable as you are necessary for social functioning. Supernatural agents who possess all of this strategic information and are apt to act on it demonstrate the acquisition of a meme based on relevance (Boyer, 2001). Supernatural agents in possession of strategic social and moral information require less cognitive effort while simultaneously yielding great inferential potential. Such memes "enjoy a great advantage in cultural transmission" (Boyer, 2001, p. 167).

⤴

Modes of Religiosity

Cognitively Optimal and Cognitively Costly Religious Concepts

On the assumption that the human brain is naturally equipped to acquire information about supernatural agents, anthropologist Harvey Whitehouse (2004) has differentiated between *cognitively optimal religion* and *cognitively costly religion*. Cognitively optimal religious concepts involve concepts that can be found throughout all religions, both historically and in the present. Because of its apparent universality, Whitehouse (2004) asserts that the cognitive optimum is a compelling attractor in human cognitive architecture to which religious concepts adhere. Those religious concepts include supernatural agents, rituals, and narratives. For cognitively optimal religion, supernatural agents are straightforward, religious rituals are easy to decipher, and religious narratives responsible for transmitting information about beliefs are simple, easy to remember, and provide a master narrative from which derivative narratives may arise. Transmission of this kind of religious knowledge involves the same investment of cognitive resources as transmitting folktales that sender and receiver know to be fictional (Whitehouse, 2004). An uncomplicated example is the story of Santa Claus. Santa Claus is a minimally counterintuitive agent who violates principles of intuitive physics by getting reindeer to fly, traversing the world in 24 hours, and managing to make himself small enough to get in and out of chimneys, not to mention avoiding smoldering embers. Typical rituals (in our household anyway) involved writing a letter and leaving cookies and milk for Santa and carrots for the reindeer. Narratives surrounding Santa Claus are best expressed in the Christmas standard *Santa Claus is Comin' to Town* written in 1934 by John Frederick Coots and Haven Gillespie. The lyrics call us to vigilance against crying, pouting, and general naughtiness because the all-knowing and ever-present Santa is always watching, particularly concerned for our sleep habits and moral conduct. Those whose behave badly end up on the naughty list. The song is a perennial holiday favorite, ensuring that the concept of a jolly omniscient supernatural agent who spies on children and then enters their homes to eat cookies and leave presents is transmitted from generation to generation.

Conversely, cognitively costly religious concepts related to supernatural agents are complicated and difficult to understand; their rituals are elaborate and often indecipherable without a guide. Narratives associated with these complex religious constructs are fragmented and oblique; they are vehicles to convey doctrinal knowledge or hints to esoteric mysteries (Whitehouse, 2004). During his anthropological field work in Papua New Guinea, Whitehouse (2004) describes his encounter with cognitively costly religious concepts among the Mali Baining. Their concepts of the supernatural and the rituals associated with it were obscure and elaborate. Their religion took the form of a secret male cult, which involved elaborate and painful initiation rituals (Whitehouse, 2004). The initiation involved the learning of complicated dances and the construction of masks they would wear while dancing, which were supported by the insertion of a sharpened bone into the skin near the base of the spine.

> Throughout the process of initiation, novices were given to believe that every detail of the masks, instruments, rituals, tortures, and dances had deeper inner meanings that only the elders were capable of grasping fully. The unraveling of these meanings were largely a matter of personal revelation rather than direct instruction, and this was expected to take place very gradually (over the lifespan). (p. 53)

The cognitive costliness of the Mali Baining religion was evident when Whitehouse attempted to interview the elders about their religion. The responses to his questions were "so cryptic as to be virtually unintelligible" (Whitehouse, 2004, p. 53). The elders insisted "that there was a system of knowledge behind the rites of initiation, evidently relating to the 'hidden' causes of human and animal fertility and reproduction" (p. 53).

Doctrinal and Imagistic Modes of Religiosity

Based on his field work in Papua New Guinea among the Mali Baining people, Whitehouse (1995) identified two distinct modes of religiosity. Experiences that evoke strong emotions, build lasting social bonds, and provide a sense of revelation are associated with the *imagistic mode*, while low-arousal experiences designed to transmit theological doctrine to larger groups of people are associated with the *doctrinal mode*. These two modes are consistent with previous observations about religion that acknowledge that some practices conducted infrequently and in a highly stimulating atmosphere evoke strong, memorable emotions, while other practices conducted more frequently and in a calm, subdued atmosphere are less likely to produce an emotional response. Imagistic experiences "tend to trigger a lasting sense of revelation and to produce powerful bonds between small groups of ritual participants" (Whitehouse, 2004, p. 63), while doctrinal experiences are "often accompanied by the transmission of complex theology and doctrine and also tend to mark out larger religious communities" (p. 63).

Whitehouse (1995) identified these distinct modes through his study of the Pomio Kivung movement, an indigenous religious movement centered around a belief in an apocalyptic era of power and wealth by "the acquisition of Western technology through the performance of ritual and a Christian-syncretic vision of eternal 'heaven on earth'" (p. 41). Whitehouse identified two groups within the Pomio Kivung movement. One was the so-called mainstream movement, which reflected the doctrinal mode of religiosity and was characterized by repetitive practices and rituals with little emotional arousal. These rituals had become routinized through performances that occurred frequently and were designed to reinforce the practice of moral behavior. One such illustration is the daily ritual involving the Cemetery Temple, which was observed by the entire community. Through an elaborate and carefully orchestrated set of procedures, food is left in the temple for the ancestors. A "witness" is appointed to stand vigil and determine whether the ancestors have visited either by making noises or through disturbing the food. If no noise is heard and the food appears undisturbed, an "orator" who hears the witness's report "urges people to consider how they have caused offence. . . . He tells them that a monetary collection must be performed soon to wipe the slate clean and restore moral purity in the village" (p. 73). The orator continues by reminding the community that reunion with the ancestors cannot occur without the requisite moral conduct. Should the ancestors visit, the orator conveys the good news and encourages the community to continue their righteous behavior and resist corruption by Satan. The ritual concludes with applause and the recitation of the Lord's Prayer, after which everyone shakes hands. The orator plays an important role in reinforcing the doctrinal teachings of the movement, while the frequency and low level of emotional arousal associated with the daily ritual exemplify its routinization.

In contrast to the practices of the mainstream group, the splinter group practiced activities that were "highly evocative of emotions and sensations, ranging from euphoria to shameful eroticism" (Whitehouse, 1995, p. 3), and as such reflected the imagistic mode. The splinter group began with the possession experience of a young man named Tanotka who believed he was possessed by an authoritative ancestral spirit. During his possession, he made statements that would be interpreted by his companion Baninge that would transform the Pomio Kivung movement. Through a succession of Tanotka's authoritative dreams, and possession utterances, along with dances, feasts, and rituals, Baninge sought to upset the status quo by supplanting the established leadership of the mainstream religion and bring about promised coming of the ancestors with their wealth and power. The mystical experiences that imbued Tanotka and Baninge with power could not be easily codified into doctrinal form nor routinized into established rituals. Whitehouse (1995) describes a climactic ritual which Baninge believed would demonstrate the imminence of the ancestors' coming. He proposed a mass marriage of the single young men and women in the village, many of whom had not reached the customary age to be eligible for marriage. Moreover, the pairings Baninge arranged violated some of the cultural norms to which the Mali Baining people were accustomed. Such extraordinary measures would alienate some members of the village and potentially provoke legal action from aggrieved fathers. "As such, Baninge was demonstrating his belief in the imminence of the miracle beyond question" (Whitehouse, 1995, p. 141). In contrast to the low-arousal, high-frequency rituals of the mainstream movement, the Pomio Kivung splinter movement imbued "the guiding themes of Kivung ideology with mystical, compelling, and emotive connotations, which verbalized doctrine alone cannot successfully cultivate" (Whitehouse, 1995, p. 184).

Whitehouse (1995) argues that the burst of apocalyptic fervor that overcame the splinter group serves to deepen the overall movement's appreciation for and commitment to the values associated with salvation. Whitehouse illustrates how the two modes of religiosity appeared to complement one another.

> Although mainstream institutions are intellectually or logically persuasive, they are not productive of an intense yearning for the millennium. Climactic rituals, by contrast, cultivate compelling and moving images of eschatological themes ... combing the revelation of these images with an experience and expression of solidarity, awe, suffering, mystery, and suspense. This gamut of emotions and sensations becomes associated in the minds of cultists with the central project of the movement. Splinter-group activities are intrinsically temporary and commitment to the mainstream Pomio Kivung is typically restored. Nevertheless, the intensity of climactic rituals, and the simplicity and power of their iconic imagery, render them highly memorable, so that they haunt and reverberate with the humdrum repetitions of mainstream religion for years to come. (p. 184)

One notable demonstration of the doctrinal mode of religiosity may be found in the *Rule of Saint Benedict*, written by the eponymous monk who is considered by many to be the father of Western monasticism (Clarke, 1931).[2] The *Rule* outlines the precise conduct of the monastic offices, the number of psalms to be said during the night hours, the order in which the psalms should be said, how the order of worship should change due to the season, instructions for those working in the kitchen, the quantity of food and drink consumed by the brethren, and the hours at which the brethren would have their meals. The following is a portion from the chapter of the *Rule* entitled "How the Monks Are to Sleep."

> Let them sleep singly in separate beds. Let them receive bedding suitable to their manner of life, at the discretion of the abbot. If it can be done, let all sleep in one room: but if their number does not allow of this, let them repose by tens or by twenties with their seniors who have charge of them. Let a candle burn continually in the dormitory until morning. (Saint Benedict, Locations 963–966)

The author of the preface for the Kindle edition of the *Rule*, W. K. Lowther Clarke, acknowledged the repetitiveness of the Offices, which were to be sung at regular intervals throughout the day and night. Anticipating Whitehouse's description of the doctrinal mode, Clarke wrote, "If we find the Bible dull, the Psalms, *Te Deum* and *Magnificat* uninspiring, there is something wrong with us, not with the Offices" (Kindle Locations 127–134).

In an illustration of the imagistic mode, we turn to the snake-handling Christian sects of Appalachia. The journalist Dennis Covington went to Sand Mountain in Alabama to investigate a sensational story about a snake-handling pastor who tried to kill his wife with poisonous snakes. He published his experiences in the book *Salvation on Sand Mountain* (Covington, 2009). Covington attended worship services at "The Church of Jesus with Signs Following" where he both witnessed and participated in the services, even taking up the snake himself. As an illustration of the imagistic mode of religiosity, Covington recorded the following scene from a service outside under a brush arbor, where a small group of worshipers were gathered. Covington focused on one worshiper, a woman named Aline.

> Her back was to us. Her hands were in the air, and she was rocking slowly from side to side, her face upturned and her voice quavering, "Akiii, akiii, akiii. Akiii, akiii, akiii . . ." It was the strangest sound I had ever heard. At first, it did not seem human. It sounded like the voice of a rare night bird, or some tiny feral mammal. And then the voice got louder, mounting up on itself, until it started to sound like that of a child who was lost and in great pain. But even as the hairs on my arm started to stand on end, the voice turned into something else, a sound that had pleasure in it as well as torment. Ecstasy, I would learn later, is excruciating. (pp. 78–79)

The transmission of religious concepts involves memory, one of the fundamental cognitive processes we possess. Cognitive psychologists differentiate between two memory systems: the implicit and explicit (Kellogg, 2012). Implicit, or procedural, memory is so-called because much of its contents involve automatic responses that "reflect knowing how to respond to the world" (Kellogg, 2012, p. 128). Explicit (or declarative) memory involves what we have acquired from our interaction with our environment, past and present. Explicit memory is further divided into two subsystems: *semantic* and *episodic*. Semantic memory consists of facts, concepts, and general knowledge about the world, while episodic memory consists of specific life experiences that tend to be memorable and be associated with some level of emotion (Whitehouse, 2004). Both semantic and episodic memory systems have corresponding roles to play in the doctrinal and imagistic modes of religion.

In the doctrinal mode, "ritual action tends to be highly routinized, facilitating the storage of elaborate and conceptually complex religious teachings in semantic memory, but also activating implicit memory in the performance of most ritual procedures" (Whitehouse, 2004, pp. 65–66). Of central importance to the doctrinal mode is the high frequency with which doctrines are taught and rituals performed. The frequency with which doctrine is communicated implies the need for specialists who are particularly skilled in communicating doctrine in a winsome, persuasive way. Whitehouse (2004) notes:

> Most religious traditions of this sort have celebrated leaders who may take the form of gurus, messiahs, prophets, divine kinds, high priests, mediums, visionaries, disciples, or simply great evangelists or missionaries. The very fact that there are so many different types of, and terms for, religious leadership is an index of how widespread and important the phenomenon is. (p. 67)

Whitehouse also notes that repetition and leadership also provide opportunities for reinforcing orthodoxy and suppressing unorthodox deviations from stated doctrine. Moreover, reinforcement of orthodoxy may be more efficiently managed through the centralization of religious authority, leading to the development of a professional class of sanctioned authorities. With the professional class come institutions of learning, like seminaries, that provide the education needed for students to become sanctioned as part of the professional class of religious leaders. Moreover, the centralization and presence of professional leadership contributes to the spread of the religion. Both Pope John Paul II and Mother Theresa were sanctioned professional leaders under the auspices of the Roman Catholic Church and both gained a worldwide forum for transmitting their beliefs.

Two other characteristics of the doctrinal mode and memory are important to note. First, the repetition of rituals eventually leads to the storage of ritual behavior in implicit memory, where it is not easily available for conscious reflection. Whitehouse (2004) contends that the activation of implicit memory for the performance of religious ritual also enhances the salience of doctrinal content in explicit semantic memory, discouraging unauthorized deviations across the community of believers. Second, the predominant use of semantic memory for doctrinal information "means that the knowledge itself becomes separate from particular episodes in which it is acquired" (p. 69). This facilitates the development of a set of ritual protocols and belief system that individuals across the adherent population share; there is little reliance on the emotional salience of a particular religious episode shared by a small group of people to transmit religious information.

The imagistic mode of religiosity contrasts sharply with the doctrinal mode. The imagistic mode involves the infrequent repetition of emotionally evocative rituals that activate episodic memory. "It appears to be a combination of episodic distinctiveness, emotionality, and consequentiality that together result in lasting autobiographical memories" (Whitehouse, 2004, p. 70). Those participating in these rituals share the intense memories, encouraging a strong sense of group cohesiveness that often results in the formation of small, exclusive religious communities. The

Mali Baining people with whom Whitehouse worked have a religion that exemplifies this characteristic of the imagistic mode.

A key characteristic of the imagistic mode involves what Whitehouse calls *spontaneous exegetical reflection*, a phenomenon resulting from the high-arousal experience that produces experiences of idiosyncratic inspiration or revelation. "The key to understanding this lies in the fact that episodic memory is a type of explicit memory. This means that rare, climatic rituals are processed at a conscious level" (p. 72). As participants reflect on these highly memorable and evocative experiences, a meaningful interpretation (exegesis) is stored in semantic memory, available for declaration. The idiosyncratic nature of spontaneous exegetical reflection results in a diversity of interpretations, where agreement tends to focus more on the procedural aspects of the experience instead of its meaning. As a result, there is no doctrinal orthodoxy, no need for leadership articulating and monitoring the orthodox position, and no centralization of religious authority. These factors inhibit further transmission of religious concepts to others. Without having participated in the experience, outsiders are unable to become part of the exclusive community (Whitehouse, 2004).

Whitehouse's experience with the Mali Baining people and the two manifestations of the Pomio Kivung movement suggested thirteen variables that differentiated the doctrinal and imagistic modes of religiosity. Table 6.1 provides a brief overview of these variables.

Whitehouse (1995) identifies the style of codification, or how beliefs and practices are formalized into a code or system, as a key variable in determining the mode of religiosity. It is the first domino in the line of variables. If language is the method for codification, then it must be repeated frequently and routinized in some ritual form of transmission so that cultural materials are produced. Cultural materials based on language are organized in semantic memory, which leads to the construction of generalized schemas and allows for the production of imagined communities who are assumed to understand and embrace the beliefs embedded in these generalized schemas. The semantic nature of this mode of religiosity encourages the use of intellectual persuasion with an emphasis on a systematic form of doctrine, which in turn provides material for the persuasion and recruitment of converts. The codification of doctrine also leads to the need for monitoring and supervision in a centralized authority with leadership capable of maintaining orthodoxy. The systematic nature of doctrinal orthodoxy creates an inflexible system that is resistant to change (Whitehouse, 1995). Conversely, the style of codification for the imagistic mode relies on imagery through symbols and icons which rely on emotional and sensual stimulation to create idiosyncratic memories that form unique schemas and link ideas connected with these schemas only through loose association. Such idiosyncratic experiences are difficult to communicate, so this mode of religiosity relies on a cohesive group of practitioners who have shared the provocative experiences together (Whitehouse, 1995).

To summarize, the imagistic mode of religiosity may be described as an "array of low-frequency, high-arousal and doctrinally elusive practices that are typically associated with small, cohesive communities and decentralized structures of sociopolitical authority" (Day, 2005, p. 86), while the doctrinal mode of religiosity involves "a collection of high-frequency, low-arousal, and doctrinally explicit practices that are strongly correlated with geographically scattered communities and centralized forms of authority" (Day, 2005, p. 86).

Table 6.1

Variable	Doctrinal Mode	Imagistic Mode
How formalized into a code or system (codification)	Verbalized doctrine and explanation of key doctrinal texts	Symbolic and iconic imagery
Frequency of transmission	Repetitive (routinized)	Periodic (at most every few years
Cognitive processing	Generalized schemas (semantic memory)	Unique schemas (episodic memory)
Political ethos	Imagined community (universalistic)	Face-to-face community (particularistic)
Solidarity/Cohesion	Diffuse	Intense
Revelatory potential	Intellectual persuasion	Emotional and sensual stimulation
Ideological coherence	Ideas systematic, linked by logical implications	Ideas linked by loose associations, or connotations
Moral character	Strict discipline	Indulgence, license
Spread by (transmission)	Proselytization (proclamation to others for the purpose of recruitment)	Group action only
Scale and structure (organization)	Large-scale, centralized	Small-scale, localized
Leadership type	Enduring, dynamic	Passive figureheads
Distribution of institutions	Uniform beliefs and practices	Variables beliefs and practices
Changes over time (diachronic features)	Rigidity (permanent "breaking away")	Flexibility (incremental change/radical innovation)

(Adapted from Whitehouse, 1995, p. 197.)

SUMMARY

- Judaism serves as an excellent example of the successful transmission of religious ideas because of its emphasis on meaning.

- Judaism successfully incorporated two fundamental elements of human existence: information and cooperation. Human beings require information to adapt to their environment, and Judaism provided an explanatory framework for deity, morality, and suffering. Moreover, it provided a code of laws to govern both humanity's cooperation with God and with one another.

- An epidemiological culture (Tooby & Cosmides, 1992) facilitates the use of inference which promotes the social and cognitive processes necessary for the successful transmission of religious mental representations.

- Intuitive beliefs, naïve beliefs formed about the nature of everyday reality, are beliefs generated by our normal perceptual processes while reflective beliefs are acquired almost entirely through communication (Sperber, 1996). Successful transmission of those reflective beliefs associated with religion involves memorability, attractiveness, and the authority of the communicator.

- A contagious idea is easy to remember and has a conceptual structure that requires a modest amount of cognitive effort to understand it; it fits within the cognitive templates we innately possess for understanding our environment.

- Barrett and Nyhof (2001) concluded that their four separate experiments supported "Boyer's theory that counterintuitive concepts have transmission advantages that account for the commonness and ease of communicating many non-natural cultural concepts" (p. 91).

- Memes are defined as "units of culture, notions, values, stories, etc. that get people to speak or act in certain ways that make other people store a replicated version of these mental units" (Boyer, 2001, p. 35). Memes function like genes; genes are biological duplication programs that transmit themselves from generation to generation. Similarly, memes are cultural duplication programs that also facilitate transmission.

- Successful replication and transmission of memes involves both the *fertility* of the meme and the *fidelity* of its reproductions (Atran, 2002). Fertile memes are those memes that are successfully and abundantly transmitted, being more suited for acquisition by the modular architecture of the human mind (Atran, 2002).

- Memes generally do not render faithful reproductions of themselves. "On the contrary, the process of transmission seems guaranteed to create an extraordinary profusion of baroque variations" (Boyer, 2001, p. 38). Of this phenomenon, Atran (2002) says, "The real mystery is how any group of people manages an effective degree of common understanding given that transformation of ideas during transmission is the rule rather than the exception" (p. 241).

- Cognitively optimal religious concepts involve concepts that can be found throughout all religions, both historically and in the present. Those religious concepts include supernatural agents, rituals, and narratives. For cognitively optimal religion, supernatural agents are straightforward, religious rituals are easy to decipher, and religious narratives responsible for transmitting information about beliefs are simple, easy to remember, and provide a master narrative from which derivative narratives may arise.

- Conversely, cognitively costly religious concepts related to supernatural agents are complicated and difficult to understand; their rituals are elaborate and often indecipherable without a guide. Narratives associated with these complex religious constructs are fragmented and oblique; they are vehicles to convey doctrinal knowledge or hints to esoteric mysteries (Whitehouse, 2004).

- The imagistic mode of religion (Whitehouse, 1995; 2004) involves experiences that evoke strong emotions, build lasting group cohesion, and provide a sense of revelation and direct connection to the divine. Rituals are performed infrequently and are accompanied by high levels of sensory stimulation.

- The doctrinal mode of religion (Whitehouse, 1995; 2004) involves experiences that are designed to communicate theological truths to large groups through frequent rituals that have minimal levels of emotional arousal and sensory stimulation.

NOTES

[1] "This difference was significant, t (23) = 8:08, p < .001" (Barrett & Nyhof, 2001, p. 76).

[2] St. Benedict died in 543 AD. In 581 AD his brother monks fled their monastery for Rome and brought the manuscript with them. A specific date of publication is not available.

7

Cognitive Aspects of Religious Rituals and Experiences

QUESTIONS TO BE ADDRESSED

1. How are religious belief and religious ritual related?

2. What qualifies as a religious ritual?

3. In what ways does the performance of rituals resemble the compulsive behaviors performed by those suffering from obsessive-compulsive disorder?

4. What is the relationship between ritual and language?

5. What are the general tenets of ritual form theory?

6. What are the essential elements in rituals, according to ritual form theory?

7. In what ways does ritual form theory account for the memory and cultural transmission of rituals?

8. How does the emotional arousal of a ritual and the frequency with which it is performed distinguish between types of rituals?

9. What are the points of convergence and divergence between ritual form theory and modes of religiosity (explored in the previous chapter)?

Religious Rituals: A Broad Definition

In the novel *Things Fall Apart* (1994), Chinua Achebe writes of the Feast of the New Yam in the Ibo village of Nigeria. The Feast was a time to give thanks to the earth goddess Ani, from whom fertility came and who was "the ultimate judge of morality and conduct" (p. 36). The night before the festival, last year's entire yam crop was disposed of and all the tools and cookware associated with the Feast were thoroughly cleansed. The celebration marked the beginning of a time of plenty; "the new year must begin with tasty, fresh yams" (Achebe, 1994, p. 36). In his account of a small Southern sect of Pentecostal Christians in *Salvation on Sand Mountain* (2009), Dennis Covington describes how believers routinely handle deadly rattlesnakes as a demonstration of faith and obedience to a passage in the last chapter of the Gospel of Mark:

> And these signs will accompany those who believe: in my name they will cast out demons; they will speak in new tongues; they will pick up serpents with their hands; and if they drink any deadly poison, it will not hurt them; they will lay their hands on the sick, and they will recover. (Mark 16:17–18 ESV)

One of the five pillars of Islam is the recitation of the *Shahadah*: "There is no god but God, and Muhammad is His Prophet." Over the course of their life "a Muslim must say the *Shahadah* correctly at least once, slowly, thoughtfully, aloud, with full understanding and with heartfelt conviction" (Smith, 1958/1991, p. 244). Though only required once, Muslims frequently recite the *Shahadah* as a means of assurance or to quell strong, undesirable emotions (Smith, 1958/1991). Similarly, in auditoriums and gymnasiums across the United States in late spring, graduating high school and college seniors clad in cap and gown have been processing to Sir Edward Elgar's *Pomp and Circumstance March No. 1 in D* since 1905.

How do the first three experiences described above differ from the fourth? The Feast of the New Yam, taking up the snake, and the *Shahadah* are all *religious* rituals, while playing *Pomp and Circumstance*, for all the solemnity associated with it, is not. Religious rituals are actions that involve the performer, the object of the action (person or other entity), a supernatural agent or agents, and an outcome that would not be expected to intuitively follow from the action (Barrett, 2004; Lawson & McCauley, 1990; McCauley & Lawson, 2002). The Pentecostal practice of snake-handling illustrates this definition. The performer is whichever believer is moved by the Holy Spirit, either by faith or through an altered state of consciousness called *the anointing* (Hood & Williamson, 2008) to take up the snake. The entity that is acted upon is the snake, the supernatural agent involved is the Holy Spirit, and the unexpected outcomes include remaining unbitten while handling a venomous serpent and, for those receiving the anointing, the assumption of an ecstatic trance state (Hood & Williamson, 2008).

Religious belief and ritual are complementary, each informing and elaborating on the other; they are two halves that constitute a whole (Winzeler, 2012). The ritual aspect of religion involves actions, including utterances, that are predictable and repetitive and that are performed to worship, commemorate, instruct, and reinforce the faith commitment of those participating (Johnstone, 2007). Religious rituals are characterized by the performance of a sequence of actions or utterances that, in some instances, must be performed correctly to yield the desired results (Winzeler, 2012). The importance of precision in the performance of these rituals is partly the reason for the emergence of a specialist class that either performs or supervises the ritual in order to ensure its accuracy and to avoid offending the supernatural agent for whom the ritual is performed (Winzeler, 2012). The practice of "fencing the Lord's Table" for the Christian sacrament of communion demonstrates the importance of precision. *The Book of Church Order* published by the Presbyterian Church in America (2014) provides an admonition to prevent the "ignorant and scandalous" from being admitted to the Lord's Table. This is in keeping with the Apostle Paul's admonition: "Whoever, therefore, eats the bread or drinks the cup of the Lord in an unworthy manner will be guilty concerning the body and blood of the Lord" (1 Corinthians 11:27, ESV).

Boyer (2001) describes a ritual as a carefully prescribed and orchestrated experience that allows participants to commune with gods or spirits in a supernatural realm, often accompanied with a strong, memorable emotional experience and with the intent to procure a beneficial outcome. Boyer (2001) also identifies five elements that differentiate rituals from ordinary behavior. First, participants in rituals have specific parts to play. In the example of the Lord's Supper previously described, the pastor recites prescribed words from 1 Corinthians 11 and oversees the distribution of the bread and cup or participants come forward to receive them. Second, there is a prescribed place in which the ritual occurs. Third, there is a prescribed protocol for performing the ritual; improper or incorrect observance of the manner in which the ritual is conducted could render it ineffective or offend the god(s) for whom the ritual is intended. Fourth, there are specific instruments involved in the ritual. The rings exchanged in most wedding ceremonies or the wine glass broken under the foot of the bridegroom in a Jewish wedding serve as examples of ritual instruments. Fifth, rituals have a prescribed script that details the sequence of actions that must be followed in order for the ritual to be efficacious. For example, "one is not allowed to behead the goat and then bless it" (Boyer, 2001, p. 232).

Winzeler (2012) identifies five common types of ritual: (1) healing, which includes rituals accompanying physical efforts to heal or solely spiritual means, like the laying on of hands or exorcism; (2) subsistence, which involves rituals related to fertility, the success of the hunt or catch, or the crop yield; (3) rituals related to the calendar that are observed regularly; (4) rites of passage, which involve a transition from one state to another, like marriage or passing into adulthood; (5) a pilgrimage, which he defines as "a ritual journey to a sacred place in order to request supernatural aid, fulfill a vow, accumulate merit, meet a requirement, express devotion, or several or all of these" (p. 134). Though rituals vary widely across cultures, Boyer (2001) observed two common elements: one involves the demarcation of boundaries, specifically the setting apart of holy spaces; the second involves purification and the avoidance of pollution. The rules and regulations provided for the Jewish tabernacle described in Exodus 40:1–11 illustrate the importance of boundary-setting. The Ark of the Testimony was to be placed in the tabernacle and screened with a veil, and then the tabernacle and all that was in it, including its furniture, was to become consecrated through the anointing of oil. Purification is demonstrated through instructions given by God to Moses for the cleansing of the Levites in the Old Testament book of Numbers. God's instructions to Moses were to "sprinkle the water of purification upon them, and let them go with a razor over all their body, and wash their clothes and cleanse themselves" (Numbers 8:7b, ESV). Winzeler (2012) lists several specific ritual actions he has observed as an anthropologist, including prayers, spells, offerings, sacrifices, divination (attempts to foretell the future), the ritual sharing of food or drink, trance states, spirit possession, and exorcism.

Boyer (2001) suggests that ritual actions may result as by-products of human cognitive architecture. Rituals have specific characteristics that differentiate them from other kinds of actions and, as such, solve problems presented by the way human minds are organized. First, Boyer (2001) notes that participants in rituals demonstrate an intuitive sense that they must be performed according to a prescribed sequence, which, if not followed, would invite tragedy. This belief fosters a sense of urgency among the participants that makes the correct performance of the ritual of singular concern. The adherence to a prescribed method of execution and the harm-avoidance believed to be involved in the ritual's correct performance are similar to symptoms observed in obsessive-compulsive disorder (OCD) (Fiske & Haslam, 1997). Obsessive-compulsive disorder is an anxiety disorder characterized by intrusive, repetitive, and alarming thoughts that are anxiety-provoking, typically involving contamination, danger, catastrophe, or blasphemy. Sufferers perform certain compulsive behaviors that they believe prevents the feared event from occurring and helps reduce the anxiety associated with the danger embedded in the obsessive thoughts. For example, someone with OCD may manage the anxiety associated with having a house fire by repeating a doorknob-touching ritual before leaving the house. Although there is no apparent connection between touching doorknobs and avoiding house fires, the sufferer has come to associate the behavior with the absence of catastrophe. The ritual has become entrenched and failure to perform it escalates the sense of urgency associated with anxiety to an intolerable level.

Fiske and Haslam (1997) sampled rituals from 52 cultures and found that "the same actions and thoughts that characterize OCD are also prevalent in a sample of meaningful social rituals" (p. 211), suggesting that both involve similar cognitive and emotional mechanisms. Fiske and Haslam (1997) found that OCD features were more prevalent in cultural rituals than in other normal day-to-day activities; OCD features also occurred more frequently in rituals than other symptoms of psychological disorders. Though rituals and OCD features are similar in appearance, they differ significantly. Ritual participants have intentional control in the performance of the ritual; the rituals involve social coordination, and are infused with meaning. "People perform cultural rituals on socially appropriate occasions, in a socially appropriate manner, and usually in conjunction with others" (Fiske & Haslam, 1997, p. 212). By contrast, people with OCD feel they have no control over the performance of their compulsion, the compulsive behavior is idiosyncratic and "the private meanings they may give to their symptoms do not make sense to other people in their communities" (Fiske & Haslam, 1997, p. 212).

Boyer (2001) suggests that the same cognitive processes involved with rituals also trigger the scripts involved in avoidance of contagion, as evidenced by rituals associated with cleansing, purification, and separating sacred spaces from the rest of the world. For those suffering with OCD, ritual performance becomes pathologically hyperactivated, though with OCD rituals are no longer connected with the "social processes that usually organize, coordinate, and direct them" (Fiske & Haslam, 1997, p. 212). Similarly, Whitehouse (2004) notes that "a system that is alert to the presence of such dangers [contaminants], that carries emotional force (fear and revulsion), and that encourages the learning of contamination-avoidance procedures . . . would certainly have been adaptive" (p. 34). These cognitive modules associated with contamination-avoidance suggest "that people are naturally susceptible to learning and copying ritual procedures" (p. 34).

〜

Ritual and Language

Lawson and McCauley (1990) explored the relationship between religious ritual and language and identified several theories that explore the relationship between the two. One theory involves *performative utterances* in the rituals of nonliterate cultures. The theory was initially offered by J. L. Austin (1962), who suggested that saying certain phrases or statements is to perform an action. These utterances are in contradistinction to statements that report or describe something (Ray, 1973). Among the examples Austin gives of performative utterances are the naming of a ship and bequeathing of an object to someone in a will. Naming the shape doesn't describe it or report on it, it actually gives the ship a name. Benjamin Ray (1973) applied Austin's theory to the use of ritual language among the Dinka people of the Sudan and the Dogon people of Mali. Ray describes how performative utterances figure prominently in the healing ritual of a young Dinka man suffering from tuberculosis:

> [The young man's uncle] invokes his totemic divinity[1] and family ancestors to witness to his "words" and to join in the affirmations he makes. As he speaks, he emphasizes each phrase with a downward thrust of his sacred fishing spear over the head of the sacrificial animal, an ox called *malith*. Each phrase is also taken up and repeated by the gathered group of relatives and friends. (p. 20)

The ritual continues with a priest of the sacred fishing spear delivering a second speech, emphasizing that healing will be accomplished "through the force of his verbal command" (Ray, 1973, p. 21). Further on, the priest calls upon the priestly god Flesh to help to separate the spirit of illness from the young man. The priest concludes by beseeching Flesh to "*Wuu* away the sickness!" With this, "the people make a 'wuuing' sound and throw their heads and arms in a bodily gesture toward the land of the non-Dinka tribes to the south, as if to send the illness there" (p. 21). Although the ceremony concludes with the sacrifice of the ox, the power of the ritual is embedded in the speech acts that call forth the spirit of the illness and declare the young man healed (Lawson & McCauley, 1990). Lawson and McCauley critique the role of performative utterances in ritual as inadequately accounting for the broader role of ritual action.

A second theory cited by Lawson and McCauley involves ritual as a vehicle for the transmission of information (Leach, 1976). Ritual action is analogous to linguistic communication in that both involve a sender, a message, and a receiver who decodes the information. Leach (1976) offers the practice of brides dressing in white and widows dressing in black as illustrations of his theory. "A bride is entering a marriage, a widow is leaving it. The two items are logically related. The reason we do not ordinarily see that they are related is because they are normally widely separated in time" (Leach, 1976, p. 27). Lawson and McCauley (1990) note that Leach's theory offers insight into the broad communicative value of all cultural forms that transmit "information either from the past to the present or . . . from one group to another (p. 55). However, as with Ray's application of performative utterances, Leach's theory limits itself strictly to the communicative nature of both ritual and language and neglects their broader aspects (Lawson & McCauley, 1990).

Ritual theories offered by Ray (1973) and Leach (1976) contribute the performative and communicative aspects of religious rituals, but

Lawson and McCauley (1990) contend that these theories focus exclusively on the functional aspects of ritual and neglect rituals' structural aspects. Drawing on research in linguistics, Lawson and McCauley (1990) hypothesize that rituals are similar to natural language patterns because both appear to follow a formal structure. This provides the foundation for their *religious ritual form theory* (McCauley & Lawson, 2002).

Ritual Form Theory

Religious ritual form theory, also known as religious ritual competence theory, begins with what McCauley and Lawson (2002) describe as two crucial commitments. The first "is that the cognitive apparatus for the representation of religious ritual form is the same system deployed for the representation of action in general" (p. 8). The heart of this commitment involves the ordinary cognitive faculties all humans possess for the recognition of agents, both natural and supernatural. The presence of these universal cognitive faculties suggests that rituals will share similar elements (or *forms*) across religious traditions and cultures (Barrett, 2011). An implication of the commonality of cognitive faculties suggests that ritual form is independent of ritual content. The second commitment involves the role of *culturally postulated superhuman agents,* or *CPS-agents.* CPS-agents "in participants' representations of religious rituals will prove pivotal in accounting for a wide variety of those rituals' properties" (McCauley & Lawson, 2002, p. 8). CPS-agents in McCauley and Lawson's model are analogous to the concept of gods as understood by Boyer (2001) and Barrett (2004). These foundational commitments provide for common and predictable elements in all ritual forms.

McCauley and Lawson (2002) hypothesize the presence of three central elements in rituals: *agents, actions* through the use of instruments, and *patients,* who are the objects of the ritual. Agents refer both to individuals performing rituals and to the so-called CPS-agents. As superhuman agents, CPS-agents are ritually connected either to the human performing the ritual or to either the ritual instrument or the ritual patient. The first ritual profile involves special agents who are believed to have a direct connection to CPS-agents. The second ritual profile involves either special instruments or special patients. In these rituals, either the special instruments or special patients are believed to be the most direct way to connect to CPS-agents (McCauley & Lawson, 2002).

In the first ritual profile, rituals involving the connection between individuals and CPS-agents are called *special agent rituals* (p. 26). For special agent rituals (SAR), the human participating must be culturally sanctioned in order for the ritual to be efficacious (Barrett, 2011). In the example cited above about the Dinka healing ceremony, those whose utterances were efficacious were either relatives of the sick young man or the priests of the sacred fishing spear. Similarly, as Barrett illustrates, Roman Catholics would not consider a holy-water-sprinkling-machine to be an adequate substitute for either a priest or one's self as the agent. "The average Catholic would be suspicious of the ritual's efficaciousness if blessings were so automated" (Barrett, 2011, p. 120). In many special agent rituals, those performing them are believed to be representatives of their respective gods. In the Mormon religion, those ordained into the Melchizedek Priesthood are sanctioned to give blessings, which are imbued with promptings from the Holy Spirit and such words spoken in the blessing are believed to be the will of God (Clark, 1992). Examples of formal Mormon priesthood blessings include when an infant is given a name, confirmation of membership into the church after baptism, a specific church assignment, blessing the sick or injured, and blessings conferred by husbands and fathers (Clark, 1992).

The second ritual profile involves connecting to the CPS-agent either through special instrument rituals (SIR) or special patient rituals (SPR). McCauley and Lawson (2002) contend that most rituals in this second ritual profile are *special patient rituals*. "When Hindus bathe an image of a god, the god is the recipient of the action or the patient in the ritual" (Barrett, 2011, p. 121). Other examples of special patient rituals include "sacrifices, rituals of penance, and Holy Communion" (McCauley & Lawson, 2002, p. 26). *Special instrument rituals* are rituals where a specially sanctioned object provides the most direct connection to the CPS-agent. "When Catholics cross themselves with holy water, the water has a special connection to God (because of a previous ritual in which is blessed by a representative of God)" (Barrett, 2011, p. 121).

Recalling the importance of ordinary cognitive faculties in the practice or ritual, Whitehouse (2004) believes that our theory of mind contributes to the emergence of these ritual related categories of "agent, action, patient, and instrument" (p. 34). He offers this illustration:

> Now consider a simple ritual action sequence in which a priest taps the shoulder of a candidate for ordination with a special staff. Here, the agent (priest) also acts (by tapping) on a patient (the candidate) using an instrument (the special staff). In order for this rite to be effective, we have to assume that the priest is acting in the place a god (or similar superhuman agent). (p. 35)

In what ways do these two profiles differ? For special agent rituals, the CPS-agent through a representative is acting; for special patient or special instrument rituals, the CPS-agent or a representative are being acted on as the patient, or acted on by means of the instrument (Barrett, 2011).

The nature of CPS-agents in the two religious profiles, special agent rituals and special patient and special instrument rituals, predict outcomes from specific properties related to rituals (McCauley & Lawson, 2002). One property relates to the expectation that the actions of CPS-agents are permanent. Therefore, ritual form theory predicts the *repeatability* of a ritual. "Individual participants need serve as the patients of special agent rituals only once, whereas participants can and typically do perform special instrument and special patient rituals repeatedly" (p. 30). The role of the CPS-agent in the singular nature of special agent rituals is related to the attribution of superhuman power and knowledge given to gods. Therefore, rituals with their direct involvement would not need to be repeated. Baptisms, Bar Mitzvahs, and weddings are examples of special agent rituals that are not repeated. Similarly, the Mormon patriarchal blessing is given once in a Mormon's life by a patriarch in the priesthood of Melchizedek who has been specifically ordained to give such blessings (Clark, 1992). Conversely, special patient and special instrument rituals are not permanent and must be repeated often. McCauley and Lawson hypothesize that this is related to the mediated nature of SIR and SPR. "Whatever ritually mediated connection the agent in such a ritual may enjoy with CPS-agents is comparatively less intimate. Consequently, in these rituals the agents' actions carry no such finality" (p. 31).

McCauley and Lawson's theory also explains why the permanence of a ritual is related to its *reversibility*. Special patient and special instrument rituals are temporary and repeatable, so reversal is unnecessary. Conversely, special agent rituals are permanent and are therefore reversible. "Defrocking priests, excommunicating communicants, expelling initiates, and dissolving marriages are all possible, but undoing Holy Communion is not" (p. 31). As Barrett notes, "the god needs to undo its own handiwork" (Barrett, 2011, p. 121).

Another element that emerges from the distinction between SAR and SIR/SPR is the issue of substitution. Repeatable rituals, those typically involving special patients or special instruments, allow the use of substitutions, where special agent rituals are less likely to do so. McCauley and Lawson (2002) cite several examples of substitutions, including the use of sand instead of water for ritual purification in Islam, the substitution of grape juice for wine in the Christian celebration of the Lord's Supper, and the substitution of a cucumber instead of a bull for ritual sacrifice among the Nuer people. Similarly, in the book of Leviticus provision is made for those who cannot afford to sacrifice a lamb; they may substitute two turtledoves or two pigeons (Leviticus 5:7, ESV).

‚ᴖ

Ritual Form Theory, Memory, and Cultural Transmission

Religious rituals are structured to facilitate the transmission of religious ideas. Vital in this transmission process is the accuracy and fidelity of memory for the individuals participating in the ritual. In other words, a ritual is designed to encourage accurate and faithful memories of both the ritual itself and the underlying religious content in the ritual. The importance of memory in the transmission of religious content tends to yield two types of rituals. The first involves rituals that have low levels of emotional arousal, are performed frequently, and have the potential to be boring (McCauley & Lawson, 2002). The second involves rituals that are exciting due to high levels of emotional arousal often stimulated by *sensory pageantry*, which are sights, sounds, and smells associated with the ritual. The trope "smells and bells" is often used to describe the burning of incense and use of bells in high-church Anglican and Roman Catholic services. In addition to sensory pageantry, these rituals are performed infrequently, sometimes only once in a lifetime (McCauley & Lawson, 2002).

McCauley and Lawson (2002) draw on Sperber's (1996) epidemiological model to assert that religious rituals, like all memes, are dependent on transmission from individual internal representations to public representations, which when shared suggests that participants 'have mental representations similar enough to be considered versions of one another" (Sperber, 1996, p. 82). However, Sperber cautions against the notion that the communication of religious ideas is a simple process of a sender encoding a message, transmitting it, and the receiver decoding it and storing it in memory, where retrieval of the memory is simply to reverse the storage process. Inasmuch as biological genes may, however infrequently, mutate upon transmission, so do memes. "When it concerns the transmission of ideas, "mutation occurs far more often in cultural transmission than it does in biological evolution" (McCauley & Lawson, 2002, p. 41). Otherwise, Sperber (1996) cautions, ideas transmitted from person to person would flow from mind to mind without alteration, "with just a smooth oscillation between indefinitely repeated mental and public forms" (p. 65). Instead, ideas are transformed—much like the mutation of genes—when transmitted from internal to public to internal representations. As McCauley and Lawson (2002) note, "the transmission of culture virtually always involves the transformation of culture on Sperber's view" (p. 41). Sperber demonstrates this transformation process in his "law of the epidemiology of representation" which he applies to cultures dependent on oral tradition for transmission of ideas. The law states "in an oral tradition, all cultural representations are easily remembered ones; hard-to-remember representations are forgotten, or transformed into more easily remembered ones, before reaching a cultural level of distribution" (Sperber, 1996, p. 74). Sperber's law highlights two important points about the transmission of religious ideas. First, successful transmission is dependent on ease of recall. Second, some religious ideas must involve some degree of transformation, either in content or method of transmission, so that they may be more easily recalled. Although such transformations occur, they imply resemblance: "the smaller the degree of transformation, the greater the degree of resemblance" (p. 108).

Religious rituals play a vital role in the transmission of religious ideas. The two ritual profile forms—the one involving special agent rituals and the other involving special patient and special instrument rituals—predict both the degree of emotional arousal involved in a ritual and the frequency with which it is repeated. Sperber's hypothesis states that cultural transformations "tend to be biased in the direction of attractor positions" (Sperber, 1996, p. 108). Sperber explains further that these attractor positions are "transformation probabilities [that] form a certain pattern: they tend to be biased so as to favor transformation in the direction of some specific point, and therefore cluster at and around that point" (p. 112). Even through successive iterations of an idea from generation to generation, there is a kind of cultural *regression to the mean*[2] that occurs such that transformations do not lead to substantive deviations from the original idea. In the original Grimm's fairy tale of Cinderella, the wicked stepsisters are beautiful externally but wicked at heart, and each is punished by having an eye pecked out by a pigeon at the wedding feast of Cinderella and the prince. The Disney film version has variations: externally ugly stepsisters whose only punishment is envy. Nonetheless, the basic elements of the story remain and both are recognizable.

McCauley and Lawson employ Sperber's framework to identify two attractors in religious ritual: (1) emotional arousal as evoked by sensory pageantry and (2) frequency (McCauley & Lawson, 2002). Low levels of sensory stimulation and low emotional arousal will lead to rituals being performed more frequently. Giving an offering to a god is something that occurs frequently. In the Old Testament book of Numbers, two year-old male lambs without blemish are offered daily, one in the morning and the other at twilight (Numbers 28:1–8, ESV). Conversely, high levels of sensory stimulation and high emotional arousal generally lead to rituals where the patient-participant serves in that capacity only once. The *bar* and *bat mitzvah* rituals are coming-of-age ceremonies for Jewish boys and girls, respectively. Participants in coming-of-age ceremonies only come of age once, so repeating the ritual doesn't make sense. Moreover, for rituals high in emotional arousal and sensory pageantry, "observers and the participants in particular need to *feel* that the god is acting in this moment" (Barrett, 2011, p. 122).

These two attractors correspond to the two ritual profiles hypothesized by McCauley and Lawson (2002). The frequency attractor, characterized by low levels of pageantry and emotional arousal, attracts the special patient and special instrument rituals. These rituals do not involve the CPS-agent acting directly in and through the ritual. Instead, in the special patient ritual, the CPS-agent is being acted upon, while in the special instrument ritual, an intermediate instrument provides the connection to the CPS-agent. Conversely, the high emotional arousal attractor characterized by high levels of sensory pageantry attracts the special agent ritual. These rituals provide the most direct ritual connection to the CPS-agent, who is "ultimately responsible for what happens" (McCauley & Lawson, 2002, p. 44).

Rituals that evolve toward one of these two attractor positions increase the likelihood of accurate recall (McCauley & Lawson, 2002). The transmission of religious ideas is essential both for the ongoing encouragement and perpetuation of the religious belief system, but also for the recruitment of others into the faith. Rituals are forms of memes that accomplish this transmission without the risk of significant deviation from the essential content those rituals were designed to communicate. High-frequency rituals increase the likelihood of accurate recall through repetition. Participation in the ritual form itself reduces the possibility that the form itself will be remembered with little distortion (McCauley & Lawson, 2002), reinforces belief through public demonstrations of religious acts (Barrett, 2004), while repetition of the content through recitation and other rhetorical forms provides greater consolidation of doctrinal content in semantic memory (Whitehouse, 2004). McCauley and Lawson (2002) offer a cautionary note for high-frequency rituals: "what makes for good recollection, though, may not make for good communication. Frequent repetition may produce reliable memory . . . [however] the frequent repetition of a cultural representation may diminish the attention people give that material" (p. 50). Many of us have had the experience of reciting the pledge of allegiance by rote, not giving much thought to the content. This is the danger inherent in high-frequency rituals. They tend to breed indifference (McCauley & Lawson, 2002).

High-arousal, special agent rituals appear to ensure accurate recall by increasing the salience of memories associated with the ritual. Salient memories may be characterized by their *distinctiveness*. Memories of events that provoke intense emotions are encoded differently than low-arousal memories. "Neuroimaging studies have shown that the degree of activation of the amygdala during encoding is predictive of how well emotional stimuli are later remembered . . . emotional arousal causes the amygdala to hasten the process of consolidation in the hippocampus" (Kellogg, 2012, p. 141). Some rites of passage are excellent candidates for engaging the intense emotions originating from the amygdala. Barrett (2004) notes that "in many Melanesian rites of passage, the men of the village beat, burn, starve, freeze, cut, and otherwise torture prepubescent boys to mark their coming of age" (p. 66). The peculiarity of these infrequent rituals coupled with intense emotions of ecstasy or terror escalated by sensory pageantry enhance the probability that the ritual will be remembered, along with the accompanying beliefs embedded in the ritual (Barrett, 2004).

〜

Ritual Form Theory and Modes of Religiosity

These two attractors hypothesized by McCauley and Lawson (2002) also offer an intersection with Harvey Whitehouse's modes of religiosity (Whitehouse, 2004). As discussed in the previous chapter, Whitehouse theorized two modes of religiosity: doctrinal and imagistic. The imagistic mode of religiosity may be described as an "array of low-frequency, high-arousal and doctrinally elusive practices that are typically associated with small, cohesive communities and decentralized structures of sociopolitical authority" (Day, 2005, p. 86), while the doctrinal mode of religiosity involves "a collection of high-frequency, low-arousal, and doctrinally explicit practices that are strongly correlated with geographically scattered communities and centralized forms of authority" (p. 86). Doctrinal modes are best suited for rituals that are high-frequency with low levels of emotional arousal. The frequent repetition of rituals employs implicit or procedural memory, where we consolidate memories that often become automatic. Whitehouse (2004) notes that "repetitive actions lead to implicit behavioral habits that occur independently of conscious thought or control" (p. 68). A consequence of employing implicit memory means participants are less likely to reflect on the meaning of the ritual. Moreover, it "enhances the survival potential of authoritative teachings stored in semantic memory" (p. 68).

Imagistic modes of religiosity are highly compatible with McCauley and Lawson's high-arousal attractor. Imagistic modes by definition involve activities that occur infrequently but are highly arousing. "Examples might include traumatic and violation initiation rituals, ecstatic practices of various cults, experiences of collective possession and altered states of consciousness and extreme rituals involving homicide or cannibalism" (Whitehouse, 2004, p. 70). While highly memorable, the episodic and idiosyncratic nature of these rituals leads to a diversity of representations which in turn inhibit transmission. Moreover, the intense emotional experiences foster intense cohesion among the participants, creating a strong, exclusive localized community of believers.

Whitehouse's work with the Mali Baining people and the Pomio Kivung splinter movement provides the basis for his modes of religiosity hypothesis. You may recall from the previous chapter that Tanotka declared himself to be possessed by an authoritative ancestral spirit. The splinter movement differentiated itself from the mainstream religion by seeking a more immediate coming of the ancestors with wealth and power. One such method in differentiating between the splinter and mainstream movements was to introduce a modification to their doctrine of salvation. The mainstream doctrine made a simple distinction between the chosen people, who were perfect, omniscient people in spirit form, and the earthy Kivung, who strived to live a life worthy of salvation. Baninge, Tanotka's spokesman, claimed to have had a dream in which he saw a huge ring divided by a fence. On one side of the fence stood the ancestral spirits, and Baninge and Tanotka stood on the other. The inhabitants of the ring were God's chosen people, and those who entered the ring were guaranteed salvation.

> The semi-circle in which Baninge and Tanotka stood was to contain the living people who were not omniscient (i.e., because they were

still "earthly") but who were nevertheless "chosen by God" and guaranteed a privileged place beside Him on Judgment Day. (Whitehouse, 1995, p. 111)

This modification of traditional Kivung teaching was transmitted through the institution of the ring ceremony. A physical ring was demarcated in the center of the village and Tanotka stood alone in its midst, the people standing outside the perimeter of the ring. Each came forward into the ring individually to shake Tanotka's hand and to give him an offering of money. Once everyone had entered the ring, they all shook hands with one another. Whitehouse interpreted the significance of the first performance of the ring ceremony as follows:

> The community had now become God's chosen people and had entered into a contract with Tanotka wherein they presented him with an offering (of money) and their allegiance (expressed in handshakes) in return for guidance along the path to certain salvation. (p. 113)

Whitehouse also noted a particularly salient feature of the sensory pageantry that accompanied the ring ceremony. All participants performed the ritual with clothing only covering their genitals, which was an unusual practice among those who were part of the Pomio Kivung movement. Whitehouse notes why this experience promoted the sensory pageantry that enhanced memory of the ritual.

> First, the participants were exposed to the cold mists of dawn in their naked state. Secondly, their nakedness had a startling visual effect. Ideologically, the purpose was to demonstrate solidarity with the ancestors (who were stereotypically naked) and a renunciation of the shame which missionaries had imposed upon them. People should no longer be ashamed of their ancestral customs and particularly of the nakedness of Adam and Eve in paradise. Moreover, the rejection of foreign clothing demonstrated profound confidence in the moral fortitude of the community and its achievement of sexual asceticism: it was at last safe to expose erotic features of the body, since violations of the laws were not unthinkable. In practice, universal nakedness probably did excite erotic thoughts in the participants (especially men) and certainly produced intense shame in the women. (pp. 113–114)

McCauley and Lawson (2002) agree with Whitehouse (1995) on three assumptions related to sensory pageantry in ritual. First, rituals loaded with sensory pageantry are emotionally provocative. Second, this emotional provocation increases the likelihood that the rituals will be better remembered than it would have otherwise been had such pageantry been absent. Third, that the emotional provocation stimulated by the sensory pageantry will motivate the participants to transmit the religious representations associated with the ritual to others (McCauley & Lawson, 2002, p. 103).

However, McCauley and Lawson (2002) differ with Whitehouse on "the conditions under which rituals contain the extensive sensory pageantry that produces elevated levels of emotion" (p. 112). They differentiate their contrasting hypotheses as follows. Whitehouse's hypothesis is the *ritual frequency hypothesis*.

> It proposes that the amount of sensory pageantry and, therefore, the amount of emotional stimulation any religious ritual involves are inversely proportional to the frequency with which the ritual is performed. Performing rituals frequently correlates with low levels of sensory pageantry and little emotional kick, while the infrequent performance of a ritual necessitates higher levels of sensory pageantry resulting in a bigger emotional bang. (p. 110)

McCauley and Lawson contrast Whitehouse's ritual frequency hypothesis with their *"ritual form hypothesis*, which holds that instead of ritual frequency, it is ritual form, or, more precisely, participants' tacit knowledge about differences in ritual form that determines which religious rituals migrate to one or the other of the two attractor positions" (McCauley & Lawson, 2002, p. 113), namely emotional arousal as evoked by sensory pageantry, and (2) frequency. Ritual form hypothesis not only accounts for the role of memory in ritual, but also accounts for "why some rituals introduce sensory pageantry and arouse participants' emotions": motivation (p. 113). McCauley and Lawson believe that rituals that stimulate participants' emotions with high levels of sensory pageantry function not only to promote recall but also provide religious motivation.

The ritual form hypothesis accounts for important distinctions between special agent rituals and special patient or special instrument rituals. Special agent rituals purport to directly involve a CPS-agent (culturally postulated superhuman agents), whose presence in the ritual bring a sense of gravity and awe that would not be otherwise present in other types of rituals. Since special agent rituals are performed infrequently because these rituals are believed to establish a permanent arrangement (e.g., a marriage, an ordination, a coronation), the ritual itself must contain elements that *"convince* participants that something profound is going on. Since mere humans—limited as they are in time and space—cannot inaugurate super-permanent arrangements, the gods must have had a hand in them" (McCauley & Lawson, 2002, p. 122). Such a conviction—that a god was immanent in the ritual—enhances the memorability of the elements surrounding the event and increases the likelihood that participants will be motivated to transmit information about this experience to others (McCauley & Lawson, 2002).

The ritual form hypothesis differs from the ritual frequency hypothesis in its contention that frequency is not necessarily the primary factor in promoting memorability, but that the presence of special agents in rituals affecting permanent changes accompanied with the sensory pageantry necessary to emphasis the gravity of the agent's presence are greater factors in promoting both memorability and motivation to transmit the information (McCauley & Lawson, 2002). Even if a special patient or special instrument ritual were to be performed infrequently and with attendant sensory pageantry, the absence of a CPS-agent directly involved or indirectly sanctioning the ritual through an approved representative diminished the gravity of the ritual, decreasing the probability of high memorability and the motivation to transmit the information to others.

SUMMARY

- Religious rituals are actions that involve the performer, the object of the action (person or other entity), a supernatural agent or agents, and an outcome that would not be expected to intuitively follow from the action (Barrett, 2004; Lawson & McCauley, 1990; McCauley & Lawson, 2002).

- Religious belief and ritual are complementary, each informing and elaborating on the other; they are two halves that constitute a whole (Winzeler, 2012). The ritual aspect of religion involves actions, including utterances, that are predictable and repetitive, and that are performed to worship, commemorate, instruct, and reinforce the faith commitment of those participating (Johnstone, 2007).

- A ritual is a carefully prescribed and orchestrated experience that allows participants to commune with gods or spirits in a supernatural realm, often accompanied with a strong, memorable emotional experience and with the intent to procure a beneficial outcome (Boyer, 2001).

- Ritual actions may result as by-products of human cognitive architecture. Rituals have specific characteristics that differentiate them from other kinds of actions and, as such, solve problems presented by the way human minds are organized (Boyer, 2001). The adherence to a prescribed method of execution and the harm-avoidance believed to be involved in the ritual's correct performance are similar to symptoms observed in obsessive-compulsive disorder (OCD) (Fiske & Haslam, 1997).

- Performative utterances are verbal statements made during a ritual that perform actions and result in outcomes, like a healing ceremony where speech acts are believed to expel the spirit of an illness.

- Rituals also may serve as vehicles for the communication of information from one group to the next or one generation to the next.

- Ritual form theory is founded on two commitments: (1) ritual behavior assumes similar forms across cultures because ordinary cognitive faculties possessed by all humans are employed; and (2) ritual forms involve *culturally postulated superhuman agents*, or *CPS-agents*.

- Ritual form theory involves three types of rituals: special agent rituals (SAR), special patient rituals (SPR), and special instrument rituals (SIR). For special agent rituals (SAR), the human participating must be culturally sanctioned in order for the ritual to be efficacious (Barrett, 2011). Special patient rituals connect to the CPS-agent(s) through either their representations or representatives, both of whom are acted upon during the ritual. *Special instrument rituals* are rituals where a specially sanctioned object provides the most direct connection to the CPS-agent.

- Rituals may be characterized by their repeatability, reversibility, and suitability for substitutions. Special agent rituals are typically singular events where the god(s) are acting in such a way that makes repeating the ritual unnecessary (e.g., marriage). Similarly, a ritual that is not intended to be repeated is also a candidate for reversibility (e.g., an annulment). Special patient and instrument rituals are more likely to be repeated and more suitable for substitutions.

- Rituals enhance memory and cultural transmission through one of two means: high frequency with low levels of emotional arousal, or low frequency with high levels of emotional arousal. These two methods constitute the so-called attractors toward which rituals tend.

- Doctrinal modes are best suited for rituals that are high-frequency with low levels of emotional arousal. Imagistic modes by definition involve activities that occur infrequently but are highly arousing.

- There are two hypotheses for what determines the emotional salience of a ritual. The ritual frequency hypothesis proposes that the amount of sensory pageantry and, therefore, the amount of emotional stimulation any religious ritual involves are inversely proportional to the frequency with which the ritual is performed. Ritual form hypothesis holds that instead of ritual frequency, it is ritual form, or, more precisely, participants' tacit knowledge about differences in ritual form (special agent, special patient, or special instrument) that determines which religious rituals migrate to one or the other of the two attractor positions" (McCauley & Lawson, 2002, p. 113), namely emotional arousal as evoked by sensory pageantry, and (2) frequency.

NOTES

[1] "Totemic divinity" refers to the family or tribal god whom the uncle worships.
[2] Regression to the mean is a statistical concept that involves means and deviations. Measurements that are extreme are typically followed by measurements of the same variable that are closer to the average, or mean.

Glossary

Absolute Unitary Being The term used to describe the experience achieved by Tibetan monks at the peak of their meditation when brain processes in the parietal cortex are inactive enough to collapse the boundaries between self and the external world.

Agency Detection Device One of Justin Barrett's (2004) mental tools that looks for agency, as in the ability of an entity to act on its environment based on some apparent desire or motive.

Animism The belief that all entities, animate or inanimate, have a spirit that involves thinking, feeling, and acting. *Animism* forms the basis of E. B. Tylor's theories.

Anthropomorphism Hypothesis Hypothesis that children learn about God by projecting their experience with humans into a God image.

Anthropomorphism The tendency to attribute human characteristics to inanimate objects or other stimuli in the environment.

Artificialism A theory proposed by Piaget (1929) that children before age 8 tended to view the natural world as being manufactured. Research by Gelman and Kremer (1991) do not support Piaget's findings.

Bottom-Up Processing Data-driven processing that is reflexive, identifying shapes, edges, varying degrees of light and darkness, color, etc., which our brain combines into recognizable patterns (Galotti, 2013).

Capacity A finite amount of working memory that is allotted to cognitive tasks on the basis of the amount of cognitive resources required.

Categories A partitioning or class to which some assertion or set of assertions might apply (Medin, 1989, p. 1469).

Categorizer One of Justin Barrett's (2004) mental tools that classifies a stimulus into an ontological category.

Choice Paradigm Protocol employed at the Yale Infant Cognition Center that measures infant interest through offering choices among multiple stimuli.

Cognitive Need Capacities According to David Elkind, these are needs that emerge in each stage of Piaget's cognitive development model as a result of tension between the child and her environment that may be resolved through institutional religion.

135

Cognitive Niche   A term that describes an optimal environment suited to meet the human need for information and cooperation.

Cognitive Science of Religion   A multidisciplinary perspective on the origin of religion that suggests that religion emerged as an unintended by-product of the evolving cognitive architecture of the mind. This view is referred to as the *standard model*.

Cognitively Costly Religion   Religions that have concepts about supernatural agents and narratives that are difficult and complex and that have rituals that are elaborate and indecipherable without a guide.

Cognitively Optimal Religion   Religions that have concepts that include supernatural agents, rituals, and narratives. For cognitively optimal religion, supernatural agents are straightforward, religious rituals are easy to decipher, and religious narratives responsible for transmitting information about beliefs are simple, easy to remember, and provide a master narrative from which derivative narratives may arise.

Concepts   An idea that includes all that is characteristically associated with it (Medin, 1989, p. 1469).

Concrete Operations   The third stage in Piaget's cognitive development model where children develop a form of logical thinking that encourages orderliness and predictability. The egocentrism of the preoperational stage typically gives way to more decentered thinking (Galotti, 2013). Spans from 7 to 12.

Conjunctive Faith   The fifth stage of Fowler's stages of faith model that is more phenomenal than developmental and involves an acknowledgement and embrace of ambiguity and the recognition of truths that transcend specific ideological and religious boundaries.

Counterintuitive   Refers to phenomena that violate the expectation sets that correspond to an entity's ontological category membership.

CPS-Agents   Culturally postulated superhuman agents with whom rituals are connected.

Dialogical Religious Style   The fifth stage of Streib's religious styles model that corresponds with Fowler's conjunctive faith.

Distal Stimuli   Objects or other phenomena in the stimulus field that generate visual electromagnetic energy.

Doctrinal Mode of Religiosity   A mode of religion associated with low levels of emotional arousal, high frequency performance of rituals, and the transmission of doctrinal truths to large, distributed groups of believers.

Domain-Specificity   See *Modularity*.

Ecological Validity   In research designs, ecological validity permits the researcher to generalize from the sample to the population. Small sample sizes are usually associated with a lack of ecological validity.

Egocentrism   A normal developmental phenomenon in preoperational children who find it almost impossible to maintain someone else's perspective while simultaneously considering their own. They believe whatever they are experiencing is what others are experiencing, regardless of where the others are.

Epidemiological Framework   A way of conceptualizing culture as a facilitator for the cognitive and social processes involved in the wide and durable distribution of mental representations.

Expectation Sets   Essential characteristics associated with membership in specific ontological categories. The expectation sets are *"Spatiality, Physicality, Biology, Animacy, and Mentality"* (Barrett, 2011, p. 61).

Fairy-Tale Stage   The first stage in Harms's stage model of religious experience that corresponds to Piaget's preoperational stage.

Featural Analysis   An hypothesis for pattern recognition involving the identification of a small set of geometric shapes, called *geons*, that are put into a proper structural relationship to constitute all visible objects we are likely to see (Kellogg, 2012).

Fertility   In reference to memes, it refers to the ease with which a meme is distributed from mind to mind.

Fidelity   In reference to memes, it refers to the low level of exact replication with which memes are distributed from mind to mind, leading less to the transmission of memes and more to the transformation of memes.

Folk Psychology   Naïve, intuitive beliefs about the way the human mind operates.

Formal Operations   The fourth stage in Piaget's cognitive development model characterized by more abstract thought and the ability to imagine more possibilities beyond that which the empirically-oriented concrete child imagines (Galotti, 2013).

Frontal Lobe   Part of the cerebral cortex that contains the prefrontal cortex, an area involved in executive function, decision-making, and planning.

Full-Access Information   Supernatural agents that have all the information necessary to make moral judgments and respond accordingly.

Functional Magnetic Resonance Imaging (fMRI)   Shows active parts of the brain that contain higher concentrations of oxygenated blood (Galotti, 2013).

Glossolalia   A religious practice involves the use of a private prayer language. Also referred to as "speaking in tongues."

God Helmet   An experimental device designed by Michael Persinger to provide weak transcranial magnetic stimulation to stimulate the temporal lobe into experiencing a "sensed presence."

Gods   Supernatural agents as defined by their counterintuitiveness "in whose existence at least a single group of people believe and who behave on the basis of these beliefs" (Barrett, 2004, p. 21). Candidates include ghosts, demons, fairies, fauns, elves, and the deities of the major religions.

Hyperactive Teleofunctional Reasoning Device   A cognitive tool that tends "to see objects as existing for a purpose" (Pyysiäinen, 2009, p. 13).

Hyperactive Understanding of Intentionality Device   A cognitive tool working in tandem with the HADD that detects events as intentionally caused by some agent even in the absence of the agent's visible presence. This module is specifically mentioned by Pyysiäinen (2009).

Hypersensitive Agency Detection Device (HADD)   A cognitive tool we use to detect the presence of an intentional agent or traces of an agent in our environment. The hypersensitivity of this module is theorized to serve as an adaptive mechanism to detect predators (agents who have the intent to eat us).

Imagistic Mode of Religion   A mode of religiosity that involves high levels of emotional arousal, infrequent rituals, strong and localized group cohesion, and rituals that are complex and difficult to understand (Whitehouse, 2004).

Individualistic Stage   The third stage in Harms's stage model of religious experience that corresponds to Piaget's formal operational stage.

Individuative-Reflective Faith   The fourth stage of Fowler's stages of faith model is characterized by a significant transition from the synthetic-conventional faith into a stage that produces a greater reliance on self-as-authority rather than the external authority of others, the ability to examine deeply-felt commitments critically, and a greater sense of commitment to convictions consciously chosen (Hood, Hill, & Spilka, 2009).

Individuative-Systemic Style   The fourth stage of Streib's religious styles model that corresponds with Fowler's individuative-reflective faith.

Indoctrination Hypothesis   Hypothesis that children learn about God through indoctrination by parents and significant others.

Inference   The successful transmission of religious ideas depends on their inferential potential, allowing inferences to be made from the mental representations communicated.

Inferential Potential   The ability of a supernatural agent to explain, predict, or otherwise engage the imagination of those who believe. Gods should have inferential potential in order to be successfully remembered and transmitted.

Informal Personal Prayer   In Schjoedt's (2009) research, the kind of prayer that is associated with social cognition and theory of mind, indicating the practice involves a real interpersonal relationship with God, who is capable of reciprocity.

Instrumental-Reciprocal Style   The second stage of Streib's religious styles model that corresponds with Fowler's mythic-literal faith.

Intellectualism   A theory of the origin of religion that involves primitive people trying to make sense of an unpredictable and threatening environment.

Intelligent Design Attribution   Children tend to attribute the creation of natural entities to someone, as opposed to something or nothing.

Interested Parties   Rather than dispassionate law-givers, gods and other supernatural agents are believed to be interested in adjudicating the outcome of specific events.

Intuitive Biology   Assumptions about the properties and behaviors of living things that we hold intuitively and automatically.

Intuitive Morality   An innate sense of basic right and wrong that allows for the maintenance of an orderly society. Expectations of reciprocity and taboos like incest are examples of intuitive morality.

Intuitive Ontology   Fundamental attributes of phenomena into which certain expectations and inferences are embedded on the basis of those attributes. See *Ontological Categories* for classifications of intuitive ontologies.

Intuitive Physics   Assumptions about the properties and behaviors of physical objects that we hold intuitively and automatically.

Intuitive Psychology   Assumptions about the properties and behaviors of agents that we hold intuitively and automatically.

Intuitive-Projective Faith   The first stage in Fowler's stages of faith model where a child's religious understanding is driven primarily by the combination of religious images and symbols and the child's imagination, producing highly salient representations of religion.

Lab Effect   Confounding effect of conducting experiments in a laboratory setting where the setting itself cannot be ruled out as one contributor to observed changes in the experiment.

Limbic System   Contains areas involved with short-term memory (the hippocampus), strong emotion and the fight-flight response (the amygdala), and regulation of basic bodily needs like hunger and thirst (the hypothalamus) (Galotti, 2013).

Looking-Time Paradigm   Protocol employed at the Yale Infant Cognition Center that measures infant interest through the length of their gaze on a stimulus.

Magic The misapplication of the laws of association resulting in the belief in magic. Magic forms the basis of James Frazer's theory.

Massive Modularity Similar to modularity, except "the massive modularity model understands the human mind to be a bundle of hundreds, perhaps even thousands, of specialized devices, each applying itself to a single processing demand" (Tremlin, 2006, p. 57).

Maturational Naturalness Thoughts, emotions, and behaviors that emerge as the natural consequences of modular processing in early development. Learning to walk is maturationally natural. (McCauley, 2011).

Memes A concept originating with Richard Dawkins. "Memes are units of culture: notions, values, stories, etc. that get people to speak or act in certain ways that make other people store a replicated version of these mental units" (Boyer, 2001, p. 35).

Mindblindness A state of mind suggested by Baron-Cohen (1997) where an individual, typically suffering from autism, is unable to discern the underlying mental states of others; in other words, has a dysfunctional theory of mind.

Minimally Counterintuitive Agents Agents that have a minimal number of category violations that make them more easily remembered and transmitted.

Modularity A model of mind that assumes specific modules that perform specific cognitive tasks rapidly and automatically. Modules are conceptualized as being *domain-specific*, meaning "that a specific brain mechanism is dedicated to processing a specific kind of information" (Jeeves & Brown, 2009, p. 60).

Mondegreen Derived from a mishearing of the Scottish poem "The Bonnie Early o' Moray" (Wright, 1954), the term describes any rendering of a phrase that sounds like the original but with altered content. One example would be to mishear the title of the Queen song *Bohemian Rhapsody* as *Bohemian Rap City* (Edwards, 2013).

Mutual Religious Style The third stage of Streib's religious styles model that corresponds with Fowler's synthetic-conventional faith.

Mythic-Literal Faith The second stage in Fowler's stages of faith model where the child has developed "a more linear, narrative construction of coherence and meaning. Story becomes the major way of giving unity and value to experience" (Fowler, 1980, p. 149).

Neural Correlates The association between brain activity and religious activity is a correlational relationship, making it invalid to infer causation from the correlation.

Neurotheology The term used by Andrew Newberg and his colleagues to describe a discipline integrating theology and neuroscience toward a common understanding of the relationship between religion and neuroscience.

Noetic Pertaining to the intellect and knowledge acquisition.

Nonreflective Beliefs According to Barrett (2004), beliefs derived from intuitive, automatic cognitive processing. Analogous to Kahneman's System 1 thinking.

Numinous The aspect of reality that is separate from the ordinary world, that is associated with the Holy, and inspires feelings of awe and wonder. The concept originated with Rudolph Otto.

Object Permanence A developmental milestone that occurs during the sensorimotor stage indicating that infants have developed the ability to retain mental representations of objects despite them no longer being in their stimulus field.

Obsessive-Compulsive Disorder (OCD)   An anxiety disorder characterized by intrusive, unwanted thoughts about danger or contamination accompanied by compulsive behaviors employed to manage the anxiety associated with the unwanted thoughts.

Ontological Categories   Intuitive classification of phenomena based on their fundamental attributes. Barrett's (2011) ontological categories include: Spatial Entities, Solid Objects, Living Things (that do not appear to move themselves), Animals, and Persons" (p. 61).

Orientation Association Area (OAA)   Part of the parietal cortex that orients the individual to themselves in physical space. It theoretically becomes inactive during peak levels of meditation.

Parietal Lobe   Part of the cerebral cortex that processes sensory information, including a person's sense of bounded self, distinct from their external environment.

Pattern Recognition   Categorizing a stimulus into a meaningful object by identifying its characteristic features and comparing them with information already stored in memory.

Percepts   When retinal images are recognized.

Performative Utterances   Statements or phrases that are believed to perform actions.

PET or SPECT Scans   Positron emission tomography (PET) and single-photon emission computed tomography (SPECT) involve the use of radioactive isotopes to detect blood flow in specific areas of the brain.

Phonemes   Minimal units of speech sounds that constitute the basic vocabulary of speech (Anderson, 2010).

Phrenology   A discredited belief system that contended that "mental functioning is the result of a discrete number of faculties, each of which corresponds to a separate cerebral organ on the surface of the brain" (Norman & Jeeves, 2010, p. 235).

Practiced Naturalness   Articulated by McCauley (2011). Thoughts, emotions, and behaviors that become automatic as children incorporate them into their repertoire. Learning to write involves practiced naturalness.

Preoperational Stage   The second stage of Piaget's cognitive development model where children develop the ability to engage in symbolic functioning: "pretending to drink from an empty cup, cradling a doll or stuffed toy as if it were a baby, 'riding' on a 'pretend horse' made of a stick" (Galotti, 2013, p. 325). Language also becomes active as a socialization tool. Spans from age 2 to 7.

Preparedness Hypothesis   Hypothesis that children learn about God through innate cognitive structures that predispose them to differentiate between Gods and humans.

Prototype Matching   An hypothesis that is similar to template matching in that distal images are matched with mental representations in long-term memory. However, the mental representations are not specific templates, but ideal representations of a class of stimuli called prototypes. These prototypes serve as exemplars in memory against which distal stimuli are compared. An exact match is not necessary for recognition, permitting a wider range of stimuli to be compared with a smaller number of mental representations.

Proximal Stimuli   Retinal images resulting from distal stimuli.

Realistic Stage   The second stage in Harms's stage model of religious experience that corresponds to Piaget's concrete operational stage.

Reflective Beliefs   According to Barrett, beliefs "we arrive at through conscious, deliberate contemplation or explicit instruction" (2004, p. 2). Analogous to Kahneman's System 2 thinking.

Religious Styles   An alternative paradigm suggested by Heinz Streib that, while corresponding to Fowler's stages of faith model, eschews stages in favor of more flexible and fluid styles that overlap.

Repeatability   Determined by the ritual form, special patient and instrument rituals are repeatable because they do not involve the direct intervention of the CPS-agent. Rituals involving the direct intervention of the CPS-agent would not need to be repeated because the superhuman power and knowledge of the CPS-agent would only require the ritual to be performed once.

Reversibility   Determined by the ritual form, special agent rituals may be reversed because a god is believed to have acted in the ritual, while it is unnecessary for special patient or instrument rituals to be reversed.

Ritual Form Theory   The presence of universal cognitive faculties suggests that rituals will share similar elements (or *forms*) across religious traditions and cultures (Barrett, 2011), and involves the role of *culturally postulated superhuman agents*, or *CPS-agents*.

Ritual   A carefully prescribed and orchestrated experience that allows participants to commune with gods or spirits in a supernatural realm, often accompanied with a strong, memorable emotional experience and with the intent to procure a beneficial outcome (Boyer, 2001).

Search for Comprehension   Cognitive need that emerges during the formal operational stage of cognitive development reflecting the child's need to apply abstract thought to forming a conceptual framework to make sense of related phenomena. According to Elkind, this need is satisfied through theology.

Search for Conservation   Cognitive need that emerges during the sensorimotor stage of cognitive development reflecting the developing infant's need for permanence and stability. According to Elkind, this need is satisfied through the introduction of the God concept.

Search for Relations   Cognitive need that emerges during the concrete operational stage of cognitive development reflecting the child's need to accurately relate discrete events into an understandable narrative. According to Elkind, this need is satisfied through the practice of worship which symbolizes the relationship between the worshiper and God.

Search for Representation   Cognitive need that emerges during the preoperational stage of cognitive development reflecting the child's need to accurately articulate and reflect the contents of their mental life in symbols and language. According to Elkind, this need is satisfied through the sacred Scriptures or other forms of religious narrative.

Sensorimotor Stage   The first stage of Piaget's cognitive development model where infants learn primarily through sensory and motor experiences. Spans from birth to 18–24 months.

Sensory Memory   Memory process that briefly retains sensory experiences for further processing.

Sensory Pageantry   The relative level of sensory arousal associated with a particular ritual. High levels of sensory pageantry are associated with special agent rituals where a god is presumed to be acting.

Sensus Divinitatis   Latin for "awareness of divinity." A belief held by Thomas Aquinas and John Calvin that there is an innate faculty possessed by all humans that makes them sensitive to the existence of God.

Social Exchange Monitor   A cognitive tool described by Barrett (2004) that is "concerned with tracking social exchanges, including who owes what to whom and what social obligations must be met before something else may take place" (p. 127).

Social Status Monitor   A cognitive tool described by Barrett (2004) that allows us to attend "to the relative status of people in a group in order to determine the attractiveness of others for associations and to serve as models from which to learn" (p. 127).

Spandrel   Originally an architectural term that refers to the by-product of a necessary structure, it was used by the evolutionary biologist Stephen J. Gould (Gould & Lewontin, 1979) to describe evolutionary changes that were by-products of necessary adaptations. Religion is seen as a type of spandrel by Atran, Boyer, and others who see religion as emerging from the tendency to perceive supernatural entities that are actually false positives.

Special Agent Rituals   Rituals involving CPS-agents or their designees that are performed infrequently, may be reversed, and involve a high level of emotional arousal.

Special Instrument Rituals   Rituals involving specially sanctioned objects that provide the most direct access to the CPS-agent (e.g., the Roman Catholic use of holy water).

Special Patient Rituals   Rituals where the ritual action is directed toward the CPS-agent, as in cases of sacrifice and actions of penance.

Standard Model   See *Cognitive Science of Religion*.

Subjective Religious Style   The first stage of Streib's religious styles model that corresponds with Fowler's intuitive-projective faith.

Synthetic-Conventional Faith   The third stage in Fowler's stages of faith model is characterized by thinking associated with Piaget's formal operations, the formation of a religious identity based on conformity to the expectations of others within the faith tradition.

System 1 Thinking   Daniel Kahneman's (2011) term for thinking that "operates automatically and quickly, with little or no effort and no sense of voluntary control" (2011, p. 20). Analogous to Barrett's nonreflective thinking.

System 2 Thinking   Daniel Kahneman's (2011) term for thinking that requires you to pay attention and may be disrupted by other stimuli requiring attention. Analogous to Barrett's reflective thinking.

Teleological Functioning   The belief that natural entities exist for a purpose. Children tend to over-attribute teleological functioning to natural entities, resulting in what Kelemen called *promiscuous teleology* (Kelemen, Casler, Callanan, & Pérez-Granados, 2005). Pyysiäinen suggested that we possess a *hyperactive teleofunctional reasoning* (HTR) device that operates in similar fashion as the HADD.

Template Matching   An hypothesis for pattern recognition involving matching the proximal stimulus with patterns in long-term memory.

Temporal Lobe Epilepsy (TLE)   Dysfunctional electrical brain activity in the temporal lobe that produces seizures, and can include hallucinations and intense religious experiences. Referred to by the ancient Greeks as the "sacred disease."

Theory of Mind   A developmental process involving the ability to imagine what others are thinking, feeling, intending, etc. The ability to attribute a theory of mind to perceived supernatural entities is one cognitive faculty that contributes to the development of religious belief.

Top-Down Processing   Concept-driven processing that begins with information in long-term memory that predispose us to perceive what we expect to perceive.

Typicality Effect   Categorization based on the number of features typical of members of the category.

Undifferentiated Faith   A pre-stage in Fowler's stages of faith model that involves how the infant's earliest experiences provide a foundation for later forming concepts about God and meaningful others.

Universalizing Faith   The sixth and final stage of Fowler's stages of faith model that is more phenomenal than developmental. It is rare and "involves a oneness with the power of being or God, as well as commitment to love, justice, and overcoming oppression and violence" (Hood, Hill, & Spilka, 2009, p. 84).

Bibliography

Achebe, C. (1994). *Things fall apart*. New York: Anchor.

Adams, D. (2005). *Life, the universe, and everything*. New York: Del Rey Books.

Anderson, J. R. (2010). *Cognitive psychology and its implications* (7th ed.). New York: Worth Publishers.

Atran, S. (2002). *In gods we trust: The evolutionary landscape of religion*. New York: Oxford University Press.

Austin, J. L. (1962). *How to do things with words*. Oxford, UK: Clarendon Press.

Azari, N. P., & Birnbacher, D. (2004). The role of cognition and feeling in religious experience. *Zygon*, 39, 901–917.

Azari, N. P., Missimer, J., & Seitz, R. J. (2005). Religious experience and emotion: Evidence for distinctive cognitive neural patterns. *The International Journal for the Psychology of Religion*, 15, 263–281.

Azari, N. P., Nickel, J., Wunderlich, G., Niedeggen, M., Hefter, H., Tellman, L., et al. (2001). Neural correlates of religious experience. *European Journal of Neuroscience*, 13, 1649–1652.

Baddeley, A. (2007). *Working memory, thought, and action*. New York: Oxford University Press.

Baron-Cohen, S. (1997). *Mindblindness: An essay on autism and theory of mind*. Cambridge, MA: MIT Press.

Baron-Cohen, S., Leslie, A., & Frith, U. (1983). Does the autistic child have a theory of mind? *Cognition*, 21, 37–46.

Barrett, J. L. (2004). *Why would anyone believe in god?* Lanham, MD: AltaMira Press.

Barrett, J. L. (2008). Coding and quantifying counterintuitiveness in religious concepts: Theoretical and methodological reflections. *Method and Theory in the Study of Religion*, 20, 308–338.

Barrett, J. L. (2011). *Cognitive science, religion, and theology: From human minds to divine minds*. West Conshohocken, PA: Templeton Press.

Barrett, J. L. (2012). *Born believers: The science of children's religious belief*. New York: Free Press.

Barrett, J. L., & Nyhof, M. A. (2001). Spreading non-natural concepts: The role of intuitive conceptual structures in memory and transmission of cultural materials. *Journal of Cognition and Culture*, 1, 69–100.

145

Barrett, J. L., & Richert, R. A. (2003). Anthropomorphism or preparedness? Exploring children's god concepts. *Review of Religious Research, 44,* 300–312.

Barrett, J. L., Burdett, E. R., & Porter, T. J. (2009). Counterintuitiveness in folktales: Finding the cognitive optimum. *Journal of Cognition and Culture, 9,* 271–287.

Bartlett, F. C. (1932). *Remembering: A study in experimental and social psychology.* Cambridge, UK: Cambridge University Press.

Bellah, R. (2011). *Religion in human evolution.* Cambridge, MA: The Belknap Press of Harvard University Press.

Bering, J. (2002). Intuitive conceptions of dead agents' minds: The natural foundation of afterlife beliefs as phenomenological boundary. *Journal of Cognition and Culture, 2,* 263–308.

Biederman, I. (1987). Recognition-by-components: A theory of human image understanding. *Psychological Review, 94,* 115–147.

Bloom, P. (2004). *Descartes' baby: How child development explains what makes us human.* London, UK: William Heinemann.

Bloom, P. (2013). *Just babies: The origins of good and evil.* New York: Crown Publishers.

Bowlby, J. (1980). *Attachment and loss.* New York: Basic Books.

Boyd, R., & Richerson, P. J. (2006). Culture, adaptation, and innateness. In S. S. P. Carruthers (Ed.), *The innate mind: Volume 2, culture and cognition* (pp. 23–38). New York: Oxford University Press.

Boyer, P. (1994). *The naturalness of religious ideas: A cognitive theory of religion.* Berkeley: University of California Press.

Boyer, P. (2001). *Religion explained: The evolutionary origins of religious development.* New York: Basic Books.

Boyer, P., & Ramble, C. (2001). Cognitive templates for religious concepts: Cross-cultural evidence for recall of counter-intuitive representations. *Cognitive Science, 25,* 535–564.

Brooks, G. P. (1976). The Faculty Psychology of Thomas Reid. *Journal of the History of the Behavioral Sciences, 12,* 65–77.

Bulbulia, J., & Frean, M. (2009). Religion as superorganism: On David Sloan Wilson, Darwin's cathedral (2002). In M. Stausberg, *Contemporary theories of religion: A critical companion* (pp. 173–194). London: Rutledge.

Bulkeley, K. (2003). The gospel according to Darwin: The relevance of cognitive neuroscience to religious studies. *Religious Studies Review, 29,* 123–129.

Calvin, J. (1960). *The institutes of the Christian religion* (J. T. McNeill, Ed., & F. L. Battles, Trans.). Philadelphia: Westminster Press.

Carroll, L. (1897). *Through the looking glass.* Philadelphia: Henry Altemus Company.

CDC. (2014, August 7). *Travelers' health.* Retrieved from http://wwwnc.cdc.gov/travel/notices/?s_cid=cdc_homepage_topmenu_003

Clark, B. B. (1992). *Encyclopedia of Mormonism.* Retrieved from http://contentdm.lib.byu.edu/cdm/compoundobject/collection/EoM/id/4391/show/5523

Clark, K. J., & Barrett, J. L. (2010). Reformed epistemology and the cognitive science of religion. *Faith and Philosophy, 27,* 174–189.

Clark, K. J., & Barrett, J. L. (2011). Reidian religious epistemology and the cognitive science of religion. *Journal of the American Academy of Religion, 79,* 1–37.

Clarke, W. K. (1931). Preface. In S. Benedict, *The rule.* Amazon Kindle.

Coles, R. (1990). *The spiritual life of children.* Boston: Houghton Mifflin Company.

Conner, S. (2009). *Earslips: Of mishearings and mondegreens.* Retrieved from http://www.stevenconnor.com/earslips/

Cook, C. M., & Persinger, M. A. (2001). Geophysical variables and behavior: XCII Experimental elicitation of the experience of a sentient being by right hemispheric, weak magnetic fields: Interaction and temporal lobe sensitivity. *Perceptual and Motor Skills, 92,* 447–448.

Covington, D. (2009). *Salvation on sand mountain.* Cambridge, MA: Da Capo Press.

Davis, W. (2014). Personal communication.

Dawkins, R. (1976). *The selfish gene.* New York: Oxford University Press.

Dawkins, R. (1978). Reply to Fox and Greene. *Contemporary Sociology, 7,* 709–712.

Dawkins, R. (2006). *The God delusion.* Boston: Mariner Books.

Day, M. (2009). Exotic experience and ordinary life: On Andrew Newberg, Eugene D'Aquili, and Vince Rause, *Why God won't go away: Brain science and the biology of belief* (2001). In M. Stausberg (Ed.), *Contemporary theories of religion: A critical companion* (pp. 115–128). New York: Routledge.

Dennett, D. C. (2006). *Breaking the spell: Religion as a natural phenomenon.* New York: Penguin.

Dewhurst, K., & Beard, A. W. (1970) Sudden religious conversions in temporal lobe epilepsy. *The British Journal of Psychiatry, 117,* 497–507.

Edwards, G. (2013). *Mondegreens: A short guide.* Retrieved from http://rulefortytwo.com/books/mondegreens/

Elkind, D. (1970). The origins of religion in the child. *Review of Religious Research, 12,* 35–43.

Eraña, A. (2012). Dual Process Theories versus Massive Modularity Hypotheses. *Philosophical Psychology, 25,* 855–872.

Erikson, E. (1963). *Childhood and society.* New York: Norton.

Evans, E. M. (2001). Cognitive and contextual factors in the emergence of diverse belief systems: Creation versus evolution. *Cognitive Psychology, 42,* 217–266.

Fiske, A. P., & Haslam, N. (1997). Is obsessive-compulsive disorder a pathology of the human disposition to perform socially meaningful rituals? Evidence of similar content. *The Journal of Nervous and Mental Disease, 185,* 211–222.

Fodor, J. A. (1983). *The modularity of mind.* Cambridge, MA: Bradford Books.

Fowler, J. W. (1980). *Stages of faith.* New York: Harper and Row.

Fox, J. (2011). *Why "The Spandrels of San Marco" isn't a good paper* [Oikos Blog post]. Retrieved from https://oikosjournal.wordpress.com/2011/08/26/why-the-spandrels-of-san-marco-isnt-a-good-paper/

Frazer, J. G. (1890). *The golden bough: A study in magic and religion.* Accessed from https://books.google.com/books?id=9m7jBAAAQBAJ&printsec=frontcover&source=gbs_ge_summary_r&cad=0#v=onepage&q&f=false

Galotti, K. M. (2013). Cognitive psychology in and out of the laboratory (5th ed.). Thousand Oaks, CA: Sage.

Gelman, S. A., & Kremer, K. E. (1991). Understanding natural cause: Children's explanations of how objects and their properties originate. *Child Development, 62,* 396–414.

Gould, S. J., & Lewontin, R. C. (1979). The spandrels of San Marco and the Panglossian paradigm: A critique of the adaptationist programme. *Proceedings of the Royal Society of London. Series B, Biological Sciences,* 580–601.

Grahame, K. (1908). *The wind in the willows.* New York: Charles Scribner's Sons.

Granqvist, P., Fredrikson, M., Unge, P., Hagenfeldt, A., Valind, S., Larhammar, D., et al. (2005). Sensed presence and mystical experiences are predicted by suggestibility, not by the application of transcranial weak complex magnetic fields. *Neuroscience Letters, 379*, 1–6.

Grantham, T. A. (2004). Constraints and spandrels in Gould's Structure of Evolutionary Theory. *Biology and Philosophy, 19*, 29–43.

Greene, P. J. (1978). From genes to memes? *Contemporary Sociology, 7*, 706–709.

Guthrie, S. E. (1996). Religion: What is it? *Journal for the Scientific Study of Religion, 35*, 412–419.

Guthrie, S. E. (2007). Anthropology and anthropomorphism in religion. In H. A. Whitehouse & J. Laidlaw (Eds.), *Religion, anthropology, and cognitive science* (pp. 37–62). Durham, NC: Carolina Academic Press.

Hamlin, J. K., & Wynn, K. (2011). Five- and 9-month old infants prefer prosocial to antisocial others. *Cognitive Development, 26*, 30–39.

Hamlin, J. K., Wynn, K., & Bloom, P. (2007). Social evaluation by preverbal infants. *Nature, 450*, 557–560.

Harms, E. (1944). The development of religious experience in children. *American Journal of Sociology, 50*, 112–122.

Heider, F., & Simmel, M. (1944). An experimental study of apparent behavior. *American Journal of Psychology, 57*, 243–259.

Hood, R. W., & Williamson, W. P. (2008). *Them that believe: The power and meaning of the Christian serpent-handling tradition*. Berkeley: University of California Press.

Hood, R. W., Hill, P. C., & Spilka, B. S. (2009). *The psychology of religion: An empirical approach* (4th ed.). New York: Guilford Press.

Hooper, W. (1996). *C. S. Lewis: A companion guide*. San Francisco: Harper.

Hume, D. (1777). *The natural history of religion*. Public Domain.

Jardine, M., & Viljoen, H. G. (1992). Fowler's theory of faith development: An evaluative discussion. *Religious Education, 87*, 74–85.

Jeeves, M., & Brown, W. S. (2009). *Neuroscience, psychology and religion*. West Conshohocken, PA: Templeton Press.

Jensen, J. S. (2009). Religion as the unintended product of brain functions in the "standard cognitive science of religion model." In M. Stausberg (Ed.), *Contemporary theories of religion* (pp. 129–155). New York: Routledge.

Johnson, P. (1987). *A history of the Jews*. New York: Harper and Row.

Johnstone, R. L. (2007). *Religion in society: A sociology of religion* (8th ed.). Upper Saddle River, NJ: Pearson/Prentice-Hall.

Kahneman, D. (1973). *Attention and effort*. Englewood Cliffs, NJ: Prentice-Hall.

Kahneman, D. (2011). *Thinking, fast and slow*. New York: Farrar, Straus, and Giroux.

Kelemen, D. (1999). The scope of teleological thinking in preschool children. *Cognition, 70*, 241–272.

Kelemen, D. (1999). Why are rocks pointy? Children's preference for teleological explanations of the natural world. *Developmental Psychology, 36*, 1440–1452.

Kelemen, D. (2004). Are children intuitive theists? Reasoning about purpose and design in nature. *Psychological Science, 15*, 295–301.

Kelemen, D., & DiYanni, C. (2005). Intuitions about origins: Purpose and intelligent design in children's reasoning about nature. *Journal of Cognition and Development, 6*, 3–31.

Kelemen, D., & Rosset, E. (2009). The human function compunction: Teleological explanation in adults. *Cognition, 111*, 138–143.

Kelemen, D., Casler, K., Callanan, M. A., & Pérez-Granados, D. R. (2005). Why things happen: Teleological explanation in parent-child conversations. *Developmental Psychology*, 41, 251–264.

Kellogg, R. T. (2012). *Cognitive psychology*. Thousand Oaks, CA: Sage.

Kelly, M. H. and Keil, F. C. (1985). The more things change. . . . Metamorphoses and conceptual structures. *Cognitive Science*, 9, 403–416.

Kirk, R. (2007). *The secret commonwealth: Of elves, fauns, and fairies*. New introduction by Marina Warner. New York: NYRB Classics.

Kirkpatrick, L. (2005). *Attachment, evolution, and the psychology of religion*. New York: The Guilford Press.

Kirkpatrick, L., & Shaver, P. R. (1990). Attachment theory and religion: Childhood attachments, religious beliefs, and conversion. *Journal for the Scientific Study of Religion*, 29, 315–334.

Kunin, S. D., & Miles-Watson, J. (Eds.). (2006). *Theories of religion: A reader*. New Brunswick, NJ: Rutgers University Press.

Lawson, E. T., & McCauley, R. N. (1990). *Rethinking religion: Connecting cognition and culture*. Cambridge, UK: Cambridge University Press.

Leach, E. (1976). *Culture and communication: The logic by which symbols are connected*. Cambridge, UK: Cambridge University Press.

Lester, T. (2002, February 1). *Oh, Gods!* Retrieved from http://www.theatlantic.com/magazine/archive/2002/02/oh-gods/302412/

Locke, J. (1690). *Essay concerning human understanding*. London.

Mascelko, J. (2013). The neurophysiology of religious experience. In K. I. Pargament (Ed.), *APA handbook of psychology, religion, and spirituality* (pp. 205–220). Washington, DC: American Psychological Association.

McCauley, R. N. (2011). *Why religion is natural and science is not*. Oxford, UK: Oxford University Press.

McCauley, R. N., & Lawson, E. T. (2002). *Bringing ritual to mind: Psychological foundations of cultural forms*. Cambridge, UK: Cambridge University Press.

Medin, D. L. (1989). Concepts and conceptual structure. *American Psychologist*, 44, 1469–1481.

Newberg, A. B. (2010). *Principles of neurotheology*. Burlington, VT: Ashgate Publishing.

Newberg, A. B., Alavi, A., Baime, M., Pourdehnad, M., Santanna, J., & D'Aquili, E. G. (2001). The measurement of regional cerebral blood flow during the complex cognitive task of meditation: A preliminary SPECT study. *Psychiatric Research: Neuroimaging*, 106, 113–122.

Newberg, A., D'Aquili, E., & Rause, V. (2001). *Why God won't go away*. New York: Ballantine Books.

Newberg, A. B., Pourdehnad, M., Alavi, A., & D'Aquili, E. G. (2003). Cerebral blood flow during meditative prayer: Preliminary findings and methodological issues. *Perceptual and Motor Skills*, 2, 625–630.

Norman, W. D., & Jeeves, M. A. (2010). Neurotheology: Avoiding a reinvented phrenology. *Perspectives on Science and Christian Faith*, 62, 235–251.

Ogata, A., & Miyakawa, T. (1998). Religious experience in epileptic patients with a focus on ictus-related episodes. *Psychiatry and Clinical Neurosciences*, 52, 321–325.

Otto, R. (2006). The idea of the holy. In S. D. Kunin, & J. Miles-Watson (Eds.), *Theories of religion: A reader* (pp. 78–85). New Brunswick, NJ: Rutgers University Press.

Pals, D. L. (2006). *Eight theories of religion*. Oxford: Oxford University Press.

Persinger, M. A. (1983). Religious and mystical experiences as artifacts of temporal lobe function: A general hypothesis. *Perceptual and Motor Skills*, 57, 1255–1262.

Persinger, M. A. (1984). Striking EEG profiles form single episodes of glossolalia and transcendental meditation. *Perceptual and Motor Skills*, 58, 127–133.

Persinger, M. A., & Makarec, K. (1986). Temporal lobe epileptic signs and correlative behaviors displayed by normal populations. *The Journal of General Psychology*, 114, 179–195.

Petrovich, O. (1999). Preschool children's understanding of the dichotomy between the natural and the artificial. *Psychological Reports*, 84, 3–27.

Piaget, J. (1929). *The child's conception of the word*. London: Routledge & Kegan Paul.

Piaget, J., & Inhelder, B. (1967). *The child's conception of space* (F. J. Langdon, & J. L. Lunzer, Trans.). New York: Norton.

Plantinga, A. (2007). Comment on Eric Johnson's "towards a philosophy of science for christian psychology." *Edification*, 1, 32–34. Retrieved from http://www.christianpsych.org/wp_scp/wp-content/uploads/edification-journal-111.pdf

Plantinga, A. (2000). *Warranted Christian belief*. New York: Oxford University Press.

Plantinga, A. (2011). *Where the conflict really lies: Science, religion, and naturalism*. Oxford, UK: Oxford University Press.

Posner, M. I., and Raichle, M. E. (1994). *Images of mind*. New York: Scientific American Library.

Powell, R., & Clarke, S. (2012). Religion as an evolutionary by-product: A critique of the standard model. *British Journal of the Philosophy of Science*, 63, 457–486.

Presbyterian Church in America (2014). *The book of church order* (6th ed.). Lawrenceville, GA: General Assembly of the Presbyterian Church in America.

Prinz, J. (2006). Is the mind really modular? In R. Stainton (Ed.), *Contemporary debates in cognitive science*. Oxford, UK: Blackwell.

Proudfoot, W., & Shaver, P. (1975). Attribution theory and the psychology of religion. *Journal for the Scientific Study of Religion*, 14, 317–330.

Pyysiäinen, I. (2009). *Supernatural agents: Why we believe in souls, gods, and Buddhas*. Oxford, UK: Oxford University Press.

Rappaport, R. (1999). *Ritual and religion in the making of humanity*. Cambridge, UK: Cambridge University.

Ray, B. (1973). "Performative utterances" in African rituals. *History of Religions*, 13, 16–35.

Richmond, P. (2010). Scientific explanations of religious experience and their implications for belief. *Science & Christian Belief*, 22, 23–42.

Rottman, J., & Kelemen, D. (2012). Is there such a thing as a Christian child? Evidence of religious beliefs in early childhood. In P. McNamara & W. Wildman (Eds.), *Science and the world's religions: Persons and groups* (pp. 205–238). Santa Barbara, CA: Praeger.

Satel, S., & Lilienfeld, S. (2013). *Brainwashed: The seductive appeal of mindless neuroscience*. New York: Basic Books.

Scheeren, A. M., de Rosnay, M., Koot, H. M., & Begeer, S. (2013). Rethinking theory of mind in high-functioning autism spectrum disorder. *Journal of Child Psychology and Psychiatry*, 54, 628–635.

Schjoedt, U. (2009). The religious brain: A general introduction to the experimental neuroscience of religion. *Method and Theory in the Study of Religion*, 21, 310–339.

Smith, H. (1958/1991). *The world's religions.* New York: HarperCollins.

Smith, M. (1977). Development in faith: A critical approach to the work of James Fowler. *The Month,* 16, 9–11.

Smith, J. (1986). Reid's functional explanation of sensation. *History of Philosophy Quarterly,* 2, 175–193.

Southgate, V. and Vernetti, A. (2014). Belief-based action prediction in preverbal infants. *Cognition,* 130, 1–10.

Sperber, D. (1996). *Explaining culture: A naturalistic approach.* Malden, MA: Blackwell Publishing.

Stark, R. (2007). *Discovering God.* New York: HarperCollins.

Sterelny, K. (2006). Memes revisited. *The British Journal for the Philosophy of Science,* 57, 145–165.

Streib, H. (2001). Faith development theory revisited: The religious styles perspective. *The International Journal for the Psychology of Religion,* 11, 143–158.

Tolkien, J. R. (2008). *Tales from the perilous realm.* New York: HarperCollins.

Tooby, J., & Cosmides, L. (1992). The psychological foundations of culture. In J. H. Barkow, L. Cosmides, & J. Tooby (Eds.), *The adapted mind: Evolutionary psychology and the generation of culture* (pp. 19–136). New York: Oxford University Press.

Tremlin, T. (2006). *Minds and gods: The cognitive foundations of religion.* New York: Oxford University Press.

Tyler, S. W., Hertel, P. T., McCallum, M. C., & Ellis, H. C. (1979). Cognitive effort and memory. *Journal of Experimental Psychology: Human Learning and Memory,* 5, 607–616.

Tylor, E. B. (1871/1958). *Primitive culture: Researches into the development of mythology, philosophy, religion, language, art, and custom* (2 vols.). New York: Harper Torchbooks.

Upala, M. A., Gonce, L. O., Tweney, R. D., & Slone, D. J. (2007). Contextualizing counterintuitiveness: How context affects comprehension and memorability of counterintuitive concepts. *Cognitive Science,* 31, 415–39.

Visala, A. (2011). *Naturalism, Theism, and the cognitive study of religion.* Burlington, VT: Ashgate Publishing Company

Warren, H. (1921). *A history of association psychology.* New York: Charles Scribner's Sons.

Welch, W. A. (2014, July 27). Lightning kills man at Los Angeles beach. *USA Today.* Retrieved from http://www.usatoday.com/story/news/nation/2014/07/27/lightning-strike-at-venice-beach/13250419/

Whitehouse, H. (1995). *Inside the cult: Religious innovation and transmission in Papua New Guinea.* Oxford, UK: Oxford University Press.

Whitehouse, H. (1996). Apparitions, orations, and rings: Experience of spirits in Dadul. In J. Mageo & A. Howard (Eds.), *Spirits in culture, history, and mind* (pp. 173–193). New York: Routledge.

Whitehouse, H. (2004). *Modes of religiosity: A cognitive theory of religious transmission.* Walnut Creek, CA: AltaMira.

Wilson, D. S. (2002). *Darwin's cathedral: Evolution, religion, and the nature of society.* Chicago: University of Chicago.

Wilson, D. S., & Green, W. S. (2007, September). *Evolutionary religious studies (ERS): A beginner's guide.* Retrieved from http://evolution.binghamton.edu/religion/wp-content/uploads/2009/09/BeginnersGuide.pdf

Winzeler, R. L. (2012). *Anthropology and religion.* Lanham, MD: AltaMira Press.

Wittgenstein, L. (1953). *Philosophical investigations* (G. E. Anscombe, Trans.). Oxford, England: Blackwell.

Wright, S. (1954). The death of Lady Mondegreen. *Harper's Magazine, 209*, pp. 48–51.

Wynn, K. (2008). Some innate foundations of social and moral cognition. In P. Carruthers, S. Laurence, & S. Stich (Eds.), *The innate mind: Foundations and the future* (pp. 330–347). Oxford, UK: Oxford University Press.

Index

Ritual(s)
  accuracy's importance in cultural
    transmission through, 125–126
  attractors in, 127
  boundary setting in, 120
  broad definition of, 118–121
  as by-products of human cognitive
    architecture, 120
  central elements of (agents,
    actions, and patients), 123
  common types of, 119–120
  complementarity with religious
    belief, 119
  culturally sanctioned human par-
    ticipation in, 123–124
  degree of emotional arousal as pre-
    dictive of frequency of repeti-
    tion, 127
  elements differentiating from ordi-
    nary behavior in, 119–120
  frequency and high vs. low emo-
    tional arousal in, 127
  functional aspects of, 123
  high-frequency, indifference bred
    by, 128
  language and, 121–123
  performative and communicative
    aspects of, 122
  permanence of, relation to revers-
    ibility of, 125
  precision/prescribed sequence of,
    119–120
  purification/avoidance of pollu-
    tion in, 120
  recall of. See Recall
  religious, definition of, 118
  repeatability of, 125
  role of CPS-agents in, 123–125
  sensory pageantry in, 126–128,
    130–131
  similar elements shared across reli-
    gious tradition and cultures, 123
  special agent, 123–124
  special patient/special instrument,
    124–125
  substitutions allowable in repeat-
    able rituals, 125
  transmission of religious ideas and,
    125–126

  as vehicle for information trans-
    mission, 122
Rosset, E., 83
Rottman, J., 86–87

Sacred disease, temporal lobe epilepsy
  as, 21–22
Salient memories, distinctiveness of,
  128
Salvation on Sand Mountain (Coving-
  ton), 118
Santa Claus, as minimally counterin-
  tuitive supernatural agent, 106
Satel, S., 20, 27, 31
Scheeren, A. M., 55
Schjoedt, U., 20, 22–23, 25, 29–31
Science and magic, 7
Secret Commonwealth, The (Kirk), 62,
  67
Secular unity of religion, 12–13
Selectionist models, 11
Selective teleology, 82
Selfish Gene, The (Dawkins), 102, 104
Semantic memory, 40, 110
Sensorimotor stage, 70–71
Sensory data, organizing into recog-
  nizable patterns, 34–39
Sensory pageantry, 126–128, 130–131
Sensus divinitatis (sense of the divine),
  3–4, 14–16
Shahadah, 118
Shaver, P. R., 11
Similarity, law of, 7
Slone, D. J., 61
Smith, H., 94–95, 99, 118
Smith, M., 78
Smith, W. C., 76
Social Darwinism, 10
Social exchange regulator, 64–65, 89,
  96
Social interaction, intuitive morality
  as regulator of, 65
Social status monitor, 64–65, 96
Social-cognitive perspectives of reli-
  gious transmission
  memes, 102–105
  memorable narratives, 93–96
  mental epidemics, 96–100
  modes of religiosity, 106–113

transmission of counterintuitive
concepts, 100–102
Sociobiology (Wilson), 10
Southgate, V., 55
Spandrels, concept of, 10
Speaking in tongues, 22, 26
Special agent rituals, 123–124,
127–128, 131
Special instrument rituals, 124–125,
127, 131
Special patient rituals, 124–125, 127,
131
Sperber, D., 12, 96–99, 104, 126–127
Spilka, B. S., 22, 77–78
Spiritual Life of Children, The (Coles),
70
Spontaneous exegetical reflection, 112
Standard model of the cognitive sci-
ence of religion, 11, 17
Stark, R., 5
Sterelny, K., 95, 105
Strategic information, 65, 67
Streib, H., 78–80
Strong naturalness theory/prepared-
ness hypothesis, 86
Subjective religious style, 79
Summa Theologica (Aquinas), 14
Supernatural agency, and inferential
potential, 64
Sympathetic magic, 7
Synthetic-conventional stage of faith,
77

Teleological functioning, 81
Teleological reasoning, and creationism, 85
Teleology
promiscuous, 84
promiscuous/selective, 82
properties of both living and nonliving things explained through,
82
Template and concept model, 43–47
Template matching, 37
Templates vs. categorizers, 43
Temporal lobe epilepsy, religious
experiences attributed to, 21–22
Ten Commandments, traditional division into three sections, 96

Theistic approaches
Aquinas/Calvin model, 13–15
the holy and the sacred, 16–17
Plantinga's argument for, 13
"Theodiversity Sampler, A" (Lester), 1
Theology, child's, 69–70
Theory of mind, 9, 54–57, 63, 65–67,
124
Things Fall Apart (Achebe), 118
Tolkien, J. R. R., 63
Tooby, J., 96–97
Trace-detection, 56–57, 82
Transcendent religions, 3
Transmission
of counterintuitive concepts,
100–102
cultural. *See* Cultural transmission
of memes, 102–105
memorable narratives, 93–96
mental epidemics, 96–100
modes of religiosity, 106–113
of religious concepts, 100
social-cognitive perspectives of,
93–113
transformation of ideas during,
104–105, 125
through use of inferences, 97
Tremlin, T., 49, 52, 54, 56, 58, 97,
104–105
Tweney, R. D., 61
Tyler, S. W., 59
Tylor, 4–6, 8
Typicality effect, 41

Umbanda, 2
Units of imitation, memes as,
102–103
Universal grammar, Chomsky's the-
ory of, 97
Universalizing stage of faith, 78
Upala, M. A., 61

Vernetti, A., 55
Viljoen, H. G., 78
Visala, A., 52

Warren, H. C., 6
Welch, W. A., 89
White, E. B., 56